"Ugresic is unbeatable at explaining the inexplicable entanglements of Balkan cultural traditions, particularly as they relate to the hellish position of women."
—Clive James

"Like Nabokov, Ugresic affirms our ability to remember as a source for saving our moral and compassionate identity."
—*Washington Post*

"As long as some, like Ugresic, who can write well, do, there will be hope for the future."
—*New Criterion*

"Ugresic's wit is bound by no preconceived purposes, and once the story takes off, a wild freedom of association and adventurous discernment is set in motion. . . . Ugresic dissects the social world."
—*World Literature Today*

"Ugresic must be numbered among what Jacques Maritain called the dreamers of the true; she draws us into the dream."
—*New York Times*

"Dubravka Ugresic is the philosopher of evil and exile, and the storyteller of many shattered lives."
—Charles Simic

"A unique tone of voice, a madcap wit and a lively sense of the absurd. Ingenious."
—Marina Warner

Also by
Dubravka Ugresic

Fiction

Baba Yaga Laid an Egg
Fox
The Ministry of Pain
Lend Me Your Character
The Museum of Unconditional Surrender
Fording the Stream of Consciousness
In the Jaws of Life and Other Stories

Essays

Europe in Sepia
Karaoke Culture
Nobody's Home
Thank You for Not Reading: Essays on Literary Trivia
The Culture of Lies: Antipolitical Essays

Dubravka Ugresic

American Fictionary

Translated from the Croatian
by Celia Hawkesworth and
Ellen Elias-Bursać

OPEN LETTER
LITERARY TRANSLATIONS FROM THE UNIVERSITY OF ROCHESTER

This book was first published as *Have A Nice Day: From the Balkan War to the American Dream* (translated by Celia Hawkesworth). London: Jonathan Cape 1994; New York: Viking Penguin 1995. *American Fictionary* is a new, revised edition. Dubravka Ugresic is responsible for all changes and additions. The Open Letter edition includes revisions and new translations by Ellen Elias-Bursać and is the first, in any language, to include these changes.

First edition, 2018

Library of Congress Cataloging-in-Publication Data: Available.
ISBN-13: 978-1-940953-84-7 / ISBN-10: 1-940953-84-7

This project is supported in part by an award from the National Endowment for the Arts and the New York State Council on the Arts with the support of Governor Andrew M. Cuomo and the New York State Legislature.

Council on the Arts

Printed on acid-free paper in the United States of America.

Text set in Caslon, a family of serif typefaces based on the designs of William Caslon (1692–1766).

Design by N. J. Furl

Open Letter is the University of Rochester's nonprofit, literary translation press:
Dewey Hall 1-219, Box 278968, Rochester, NY 14627

www.openletterbooks.org

Contents

American Fictionary

I write beginning with facts. I try not to modify facts. I try to link disparate facts. I may have gotten this from Lomonosov—the juxtaposition of disparate ideas—or it may come from Anatole France, banging the heads of epithets together. So maybe rather than epithets, I'm trying to bang things—facts—together.

—Viktor Shklovsky, "How I Write," tr. Adam Siegel, *Context* 23, Dalkey Archive Press, 2011: 14-5.

Perhaps history never has unfolded in a linear fashion; perhaps language never has unfolded in a linear fashion. Everything moves in loops, tropes, inversions of meaning. . . . Everything occurs in a great whirl, in effects which short-circuit their (metaleptic) causes, in the Witz of events, in perverse events (except within a rectified history, which, for just that reason, no longer is history).

—Jean Baudrillard, *Cool Memories II, 1987-1990*, tr. Chris Turner, Duke University Press, 1996: 37.

Fictionary

Every book has its own intimate story of how it came to be. The backstory remains hidden from the reader and usually has meaning only for the author. Sometimes, however, the story of how it came to be is difficult to tease apart from the book itself, sometimes the story of its making *is* the book itself. I wrote this book at a time when *all my words scattered*, like those of Lewis Carroll's Alice. By writing I have tried to put my scattered words (and scattered worlds) into some sort of order. That, I think, is why I called it a dictionary. Because only words that have been put in order can be stowed in dictionaries.

I spent September 1991 with my Zagreb neighbors in the cellar of the apartment building where I lived. War had broken out in my country. Following instructions from the Civil Defense office, we all kept a "bag with the essentials" beside the door. At the sound of the air-raid warning siren we would run down to our cellars, improvised shelters, carrying the bags with us. In their bags many women brought along knitting needles and wool.

At the end of September I was invited to Amsterdam. Throwing some clothes into my "bag with the essentials," I boarded the train on a day when there were no air-raid warnings. At the beginning of January the following year I was slated to go to Wesleyan University in Middletown, Connecticut. But at that stage America seemed about as far away as another planet. Instead of the proposed week in Amsterdam, I stayed for three. Every day I would set off for the station and then postpone my return to Zagreb with the firm intention of leaving the next day. These postponements betrayed a childish disbelief, the hope that the war was just a nightmare that would vanish in the morning as if it had never been. And then I suddenly decided I would not go back. And it was as if the decision hadn't come from me but from fear mixed with despair, despair with hopelessness, hopelessness with a furtive sense of shame. In Amsterdam I applied for a visa and set off for America somewhat earlier than I'd planned. At the time I didn't yet know that horror cannot be erased by distance. The price of distance is a daily, double portion of fear: fear for one's family, friends, city, for one's "emotional property." That seems to be how it goes. Everyone pays a price, no one gets off scot-free.

While I was in Amsterdam I wrote a short piece for a Dutch daily newspaper. And when I reached America the paper offered me a regular thousand-word column. Without much thought, I called the column *My American Dictionary*. The little column saved my life. How could a thousand words save a life? There was a moment when I had a powerful sense of being nowhere at all. Even harmless Middletown (there are about thirty with that name in America!) heightened my anxiety. Clutching at the slender Amsterdam commitment like a straw, I set up my inner coordinates across an empty space: Zagreb—Amsterdam—Middletown. What saves a life is daily routine: feeding paper into the typewriter, writing an article, sending it to Amsterdam, phoning Zagreb . . .

"Your essays are very sad: they seem to be about someone who has stumbled into a completely empty house and is now furnishing it with things, slowly and rather absentmindedly," later wrote Henk, a friend and the editor of my Dutch books. I had no idea then that the image of "someone who had stumbled into a completely empty house" would grow into a permanent sense of homelessness.

This is an indecent book. I have always believed (and still do) that a writer with any self-respect should avoid three things:
a) autobiography;
b) writing about other countries;
c) diaries.

All three smack of narcissism, which is undoubtedly the basic premise of any literary act, but shouldn't also be its outcome. And in all three genres this outcome is hard to avoid.

I have always felt that writing about oneself was a kind of self-improvement exercise, indecently tedious for everyone else. Writing about other countries, too, is a kind of cloaked indecency; it not only implies a foolish belief that one's personal view of things is unique, but reduces the irreducible to little dead sheets of scribbled paper. As for the diary genre, I used to believe it was just the forgivable sin of a cultural coming of age. The sad literary practice in my country demonstrates that the diary is, in fact, the genre of war.

So, this book has been written against my personal literary convictions. But excuses, of whatever kind, are always superfluous. This book is a) and b) and c). This book is neither a) nor b) nor c). It was meant to be a book about one thing, it turned out to be a book about something else, and written for someone else again. Even its author is unreliable. I now feel it was not I who wrote it, but a grown-up

Alice, whose "words had scattered," who didn't know who she was: one moment she thought she was bigger than a house, the next so small that she could have drowned in a pool of tears.

At Wesleyan I gave lectures in English on the Central European and East European novel, without really knowing what was Central, and what Eastern, Europe. I gave lectures in Russian on the literature of the Russian avant-garde. So it was that an English Kundera consorted with a Russian Pilnyak, a Russian Khlebnikov with an English Hrabal, an English Danilo Kiš with a Russian Daniil Kharms, and he with American everyday life. With Irka, a friend from Moscow, now an American citizen, I spoke Russian, evoking old, shared, Moscow memories. The parallel worlds, those past and these present ones, crisscrossed naturally.

I telephoned Zagreb often. My mother's voice poured out of the telephone receiver. In a nervous jumble the daily prices of meat and lettuce at the Zagreb open market jostled with the number of war casualties, tidbits about our neighbors and the refugees she had taken in, the news of the death of a dear, old friend of mine. On the telephone lines the sound of an air-raid siren competed with the names of the sundry cosmetics she wanted me to send her. Makeup is terribly expensive, a jar of face cream is a quarter of my pension, said my mother, crying. Her tears expressed fear, and humiliation, and thrill, and the awareness that in the midst of air-raid warnings she was asking for something utterly meaningless, and the panic-stricken ache for life to be what it had always been, all at the same time. I would go to the shop, choose the face cream for my mother in English, thinking of her in Croatian. I would buy the little things she wanted as though that act would bring the war itself to an end. I often called Maja in Ithaca, who called Hatidža in Sarajevo; I'd call Andrea in New Haven every day and she often called Igor in Osijek; I'd call Goran in New York who often called his mother in Mostar . . . We called each other, exchanging news like war correspondents, thousands of miles from the front.

To the exhausting mental and emotional simultaneity, this frenzied crisscrossing of parallel worlds, was added a further dimension—Amsterdam. This part was soothing, as had been my first sight of the Netherlands as I came on the night train from Vienna into the Dutch morning: a picture of light-green meadows in mist, and above—large, motionless cows floating like benign phantoms. At night, after I sent my thousand words off to Amsterdam, I often soothed myself to sleep with the poetic image of my white tubes of text springing like paper tulips out of the fax-machine into the early Amsterdam morning. The cleaning woman would contemplate my little tube of paper with sleepy surprise, not understanding the text, the peculiar little wedges, the odd slashes, a "message in a bottle."

All at once these worlds crossed and merged at an almost legitimate point, in the land on the other side of the looking glass, in America. America was gradually moving into me, at times I accepted its tenancy with gratitude, at others I would shove it out. I did not yet know that in America I was living in an inner shelter. People in shelters quickly establish a semblance of normalcy, and indeed, there was a moment when it seemed things had never been any different. It was only unambiguous details that corrected this distorted perception. That "bag with the essentials" still stood by the door of my American apartment.

This book is about all of that. So why, without a thought, did I call it a dictionary? The word "dictionary" was in my refugee luggage; the idea of a different kind of dictionary that would never be written traveled with me like a stowaway. A year ago, sorting through some old things, I found my first reading primer, dated 1957. A whole world I'd entirely forgotten was shaken out of the primer along with the dust. At the time, walls, towns, borders—the whole world described by my primer—were already vanishing. The names of streets were vanishing and being replaced by new ones, the names of squares and towns, photographs and encyclopedia entries were disappearing, people were disappearing, a whole mythology was vanishing and being replaced by another, a country was disappearing and being replaced by another, an age half a century long was disappearing. Good or bad, right or wrong, that was the age in which we'd lived: those were the letters we had learned, those were the books we had read, the objects we'd possessed, the movies we'd watched, the streets we'd walked. All of a sudden we had to change everything: addresses and address books, language and names, personal documents, identity. With chilling and unreal speed they were relegated to the proverbial dustbin, without anyone having had the time to attach catalogue labels to any of them. A whole country had been reduced to an encyclopedia entry and, like Atlantis, it moved into the *Dictionary of Imaginary Places.*

I think now that in this postmodern age the increasingly frequent genre of the dictionary, which has abandoned its linguistic framework and moved over into literature, has less to do with nostalgia than might first appear. The exercise of this form seems instead to resemble the effort of patients with Alzheimer's disease to find their way around with the help of little bits of paper, Post-its, labels, before they (or the world?) sink into oblivion. All the various dictionaries in this postmodern age are only an intimation of the chaos of oblivion.

This book is about all of that. But still, why a dictionary? Perhaps it grew out of the same furtive dread that had driven my American student David Lehman to write the sentence, "The world is fragile and I am afraid." Or again perhaps it was the same passion, entirely inappropriate to the situation, with which the women in the shelters during the air-raid warnings were knitting sweaters and blankets: pointless things. No explanation seems sufficiently accurate now.

On my return to Zagreb at the end of June 1992, I had the impression that there no longer was a reality. The state of my country, which was falling apart and vanishing, surpassed even the direst forebodings, erased the boundaries between existing and imaginary worlds, and I found myself once more on the wrong side of the looking glass. As I was retyping the texts of my American dictionary I mistakenly typed **f** instead of **d**, and my dictionary became a fictionary. The chance mistake only confirmed my inner nightmare. Because if there *no longer was a reality,* then both "fiction" and "faction" were losing their meaning. And the words I had collected in a heap had scattered again. Somewhere along the way I discovered what I'd always known: that even an accidental mistake cannot be accidental because it is certain to have already come to life elsewhere, in some other language. The French philosopher Alain Finkielkraut treats his "fictionary," his *Petit fictionnaire illustré,* as a store of those words that are just a stimulus, "a pre-text for a story."

In Zagreb I found myself once again in my inner shelter. The enormous misery, Sarajevo, Bosnia, was now throbbing at full strength. Caught in its rhythm, I began once again to sort through my scattered words. The intimate story of the genesis of a different book had begun. I also discovered something I hadn't previously known. That sweater knitted in the shelter was a deeply subconscious act of self-defense, a way (the way we know) of containing chaos, an act of white magic. As we knit the sweater, we seem subconsciously to be knitting up the reality that others are violently unraveling at the same time. But the difference between a sweater knitted in normal times and one knitted in a shelter cannot and need not be visible to the eye of the beholder. And so it goes, apparently, with texts.

These texts came into being in the order in which they appear here in Amsterdam, Middletown, and New York between October 1991 and June 1992. This ending, serving here as the beginning, was added later, in August of 1992, in Zagreb.

Refugee

"Where are you from?" asked the young Flemish photographer, in the hope that his question would relax my tense face.
"Zagreb," I said.
"And where's that?" he said casually, chewing gum.

Really, where is that? In Croatia. In a country that does not yet exist. And where is that? In Yugoslavia. In a country that no longer exists. If a country does not exist, then what is happening there is not, actually, happening. There is no death, the leveled cities have not been leveled, there are no casualties, the refugees have not abandoned their homes, and the crazed generals of the Yugoslav Army also do not exist. Everything is as serene as in a movie's frozen frame. I am at home in Holland, I am The Flying Dutchman.

I no longer know who I am, nor where I am, nor whose I am, said my mother a few days ago. That day we'd run down to the cellar, our improvised air-raid shelter, for the fifth time. Obediently following

Civil Defense instructions, we took our identity documents with us so we could be handily identified if we were bombed, and not end up as mere anonymous corpses.
When they discovered that I was going to Amsterdam, my neighbors said:
"And just you tell that Van Den Broek what's happening here . . ."
We were all sitting in the cellar of our apartment building. My neighbors were knitting and embroidering, drawing their shattered nerves through the soothing skeins of wool and thread.
"I'll tell him . . ." I blurted.

They looked at me without a trace of doubt in their eyes. Now—as I walk through the streets of Amsterdam—I know that all those sweaters, cardigans, and afghans they began are finished, and in the dark cellar of my building they are nervously knitting new ones.

In the foyer of the Hotel Ambassador on the Herengracht canal (where the reflections of buildings tremble on jelly-like water), I answer a question asked by a journalist.
"To date, more than three hundred protected cultural monuments have been destroyed in Croatia. Bombing Dubrovnik is a crime of the same order as bombing Venice."
"Bombing Venice! Appalling!"
At Artis, the Amsterdam zoo, I was watching the tranquil reptiles. In my head was a note from a Zagreb newspaper I'd read before I left. A group was sending an open letter to Luciano Pavarotti on the occasion of his recent concert for the protection of the tortoises of the Galápagos. "Mr. Pavarotti," wrote my countrymen, "the Croats are no less under threat. The Croats are the tortoises from the Galápagos."
"They shouldn't have done that," an acquaintance commented, "self-pity is counter-productive."

I agree. Death is counter-productive. The Yugoslav papers are full of open letters. Open letters to Milan Kundera, to Peter Handke, to György Konrád . . . Open letters are a wartime genre, a genre of extreme despair, envisaged as the public denunciation of another, but in practice a public declaration of one's own feelings. Open letters are a contrived and inappropriate genre: they are never read by the people they address, they are a form of public self-denigration by those who write them. Yugoslav literature, during the war, has shrunk to two genres: open letters and diaries. It is all tasteless, out-of-place, a bad joke, *poshlost*, an untranslatable Russian word as Vladimir Nabokov said somewhere, a recycling of the tawdry.

Rivers of refugees set out from the shelled city of Vukovar. One woman managed somehow to reach her relations in Zagreb who by chance lived on Vukovar Street.
Having avoided death in Vukovar, the woman went out the next day and was mowed down by a stray bomb. Her death is a bad joke. The deaths are no longer counted in Yugoslavia. Life is going for a pittance, both Serbs and Croats are dying cheap.

I call my mother in Zagreb. She's crying.
"Don't worry," she stutters through tears, "we're all crying. Our nerves are worn to a frazzle."

At the Bodega Kayzer café I drink coffee and jot down pairs of opposites on a slip of paper. Organized, the right—disorganized, the left; democracy—democratic symbols in lieu of democracy; civilized—primitive; legitimate—illegitimate; rational consciousness—mythic consciousness; facing the future—a necrophiliac obsession with the past; predictability—unpredictability; an orderly system of criteria and values—absence of system; individual awareness—collective awareness; citizen—ethnicity. I give the left-hand column the heading Western Europe, the right, Eastern Europe.

And suddenly I see her, Eastern Europe. She's sitting at my table, we look at each other as in a mirror. I see a neglected complexion, cheap makeup, a grimace of condescension and cunning. She wipes her lips, talks too loudly, gesticulates, arches her eyebrows. I see in her eyes a glint of simultaneous despair and cunning, I see a panicked need to stop being a second-class citizen and become somebody. My sister, my sad Eastern Europe.

At Hoppe café, I am introduced to a Yugoslav woman with an English surname, acquired through a simple marital transaction. I catch her scent, she's "one of us," the sort I recognize immediately. She wrote a book, "a personal story": she found herself in Kuwait, and since she was there, hey, why not write a book. My life before Kuwait, my life after Kuwait. My countrywoman prattles on. Twenty-five thousand copies in America, twenty thousand in Germany, twenty in England, twenty in Holland . . . Only the French weren't interested, the fools . . . There is going to be a movie, she says, based on her personal story. Evidently she likes the word "personal."

"Write about Yugoslavia, why not? It's a bit like Kuwait," I say.

"That's not my personal story," she says hastily. "Besides, it wouldn't be *marketable* for the media."

I understand her. Kuwait was her suddenly acquired ID card, she's not letting go as long as there's life in it. And misfortune needs good management, a brand, and a market. If the war horrors in Croatia had been designed by Yves Saint Laurent someone might have noticed them. As it is, the heap of deaths and misery "down there," in the Balkans is unpalatable in marketing terms. And as soon as it's unpalatable to the market, it's morally and emotionally unpalatable as well.

In the *Volkskrant* I read the headline: "*Nieuw offensief federaal leger tegen Kroatie.*" I don't understand the language, but I get the gist. Like Erysichthon, the King of Thessaly punished by Demeter with insatiable hunger, the Yugoslav Federal Army will first devour Croatia, then, seeking nourishment, it will feed on the rest of "Titoland"—the egg that hatched it. Finally, having eaten its own offspring, it will die in terrible torment, devouring itself. The country whose ideology until a short time ago proclaimed a prosperous future is now creating that future: a land of beggars and cripples.

While the factories in the Balkans are in high gear, spewing lies, deaths, and utter annihilation, the neighboring countries in the immediate vicinity are producing protective shields of indifference. I understand that down there we are a prickly problem, I can understand that Europe wants only healthy and congenial members in its family, but isn't it all terrible? I ask bitterly.

"Stop agonizing," says an Amsterdam colleague. "You're not your country, for God's sake!"

"Unfortunately, I am," I say brusquely and I don't know whether, faced with this fact as simple as the beer in the glass in front of me, I should laugh or cry.

At the American Embassy in Amsterdam, the official coldly rejects the young man and girl from Croatia in the line in front of me.

"Go to Zagreb to ask for your visas," she says.

"But the consulate there is closed," they say.

"We don't know anything about that," says the official, the tone of her voice putting an end to the whole case.

I get my visa immediately. I'm going to teach at an American university. Here you go, why, of course! Best of luck.

I feel ashamed. I'm a privileged refugee.

I walk through the streets of Amsterdam. At Leidseplein I stop beside a clutch of people protesting against fast food. I stand there, I, an ex-Yugoslav, I, who no longer know who I am, nor where I am, nor whose I am. I buy a little container of fast food, winking at the dark-skinned man behind the counter. "There's no food without fast food," I say. He smiles, he's "one of us," Third World, I recognize him by his expression of condescension and cunning. I stand there, mingling with the warm crowd, holding the *Diary of Laura Palmer*, which I've just bought. In my mind's eye I'm seeing flashes of my homeland—so like Lynch's soap-noir . . . Except that the blood flowing there is real. The young man who is next in line holds a placard saying: Stop Fast Food.

I take a felt-tip marker out of my handbag, and write a message on the inside cover of Laura's diary, the only paper I have. Stop The War In Croatia. I hold up the cover, completely aware of my own unimportance, completely aware of the fatal strategies of the world. Mingling with the warm crowd, I broadcast my signal. I look at a glamorous ad across the street. It winks at me as though saying: I'll think about that tomorrow. *I'll think about that tomorrow*, whispers my sister, my beautiful Western Europe.

ID

Before we boarded the plane for New York, a young official once again checked our passports.

"I've never seen one of these!" he said, smiling.

"And you may never see another," I said, taking my passport and blushing at my sudden rudeness, my impropriety, my tone that reprimanded anyone who was not *au fait* with the situation, a tone that was deeply out of character but that had, virus-like, infected my voice. I blushed at the tone that rang with the whole of my country, my Atlantis.

On the plane I began to shiver at the finality of my decision. The thought of going back was unbearable. The thought of being anywhere else was equally unbearable. I was incompatible. Over there. And over here. And anywhere else. My ID was no longer valid, my passport—no longer valid. The passenger beside me asked in a friendly voice where I was from.

"Yugoslavia," I said.
"Serb or Croat?" he asked, his expression showing he was pleased with himself for being in the know.
At last we were recognized. For years I'd watched Yugoslavs wanting to be recognized. At first we had grown up in the belief that the whole world knew about us. We needed only to cross our first frontier to be confronted with the disappointing fact that absolutely no one knew about us. That was why we nodded so eagerly when a foreigner identified us. Aha! Tito! Tito was our ID abroad. Yugoslavia—Tito. I was used to foreigners asking me what it was like behind "the Iron Curtain," telling me they had been in my *Yugoslovakia* and what a wonderful city our capital Budapest was. I was used to Swedes telling me that our migrant workers kept pigs in their bathrooms, Germans telling me about the filthy restrooms and lazy waiters on the Adriatic coast, I was used to Parisians talking about the Yugo-mafia, and Londoners about the "Ustashas" and "Chetniks," the scourge of civilized Europe . . . Ha-ha, you're a dangerous lot, down there . . .

At first I rebelled, I'd launch into an explanation, draw aside the Iron Curtain, list the republics, faiths, languages, I paraded the upsides, the charm of Dubrovnik, spoke of the variety of cultures and landscapes in our little Balkan land, went on about the beauty of our coast, the purity of the Adriatic, the advantages of the self-management system, our relative democracy, our passport that was honored everywhere, our position between West and East, our soft flavor of communism. And then this wore me down. And in any case, how could we possibly, now, prove that we, down there, weren't dangerous? How could I explain to anyone that the inane phrase *nema problema*—which every tourist took away from Yugoslavia as a linguistic souvenir—had turned the whole country into a grim farce? It was with this same conscious or unconscious phrase in mind that its crazed citizens were killing each other today . . . No problem! *Nema problema!*

I looked at my fellow traveler, I saw he was expecting an answer.
"Neither," I said. "I don't know who I am."
"Well, then you're in big trouble," commiserated my neighbor.

In New York I called an American acquaintance.
"Who? Could you please repeat the name?" asked his secretary.
I repeated my last name, spelling it.
"Ah," said the secretary cheerfully. "Is that with those little guys over the letters?"
Suddenly I felt slightly reconciled. I was someone with "those little guys" over the letters of my last name.

From the Empire State Building, New York looks like a child's playground version of Yugoslavia. Brooklyn—now that's Slovenia. The Brooklyn-Slovenes are diligently setting up their frontiers, their customs posts, bringing in their currency, which they're calling the "tollar" (not the "dollar"). The Brooklyn-Slovenes are abandoning New York forever. And over there are Queens-Serbia and Bronx-Croatia. The Bronx is desperately seeking its independence, insisting it has always been separate from New York City. Queens is not letting it secede, apparently they aim to control the whole of New York. The telephone lines between the Bronx and Queens have been cut off, communications are blocked, the people in the Bronx watch only Bronx-TV, the people in Queens only Queens-TV. And the roads are blocked. You can only get to the Bronx via Boston, and to Queens via Chicago! The federal armed forces of New York have sided with Queens, they're federal, they're army, it's only natural that they always want more territory. The Bronx is already half-destroyed, there are many dead. Things are heating up on Manhattan and seething in New Jersey. Whose side will they be on in the war that is creeping through the tunnels, inching toward the bridges, knocking at their doors?

The rest of America watches the New York war calmly, as though it were a video game. Nobody believes that the Bronx is already half-destroyed and that there are real bodies strewn about on the streets. From the Empire State Building it all looks like child's play. Perhaps that's why America is so complacent. Meanwhile the situation continues to be ghastly in the Bronx, people are still being killed, whole neighborhoods are vanishing, razed to the ground.

So which is true: what you see from up there or what's happening on the Bronx streets? Is this truly all a question of perspective? From the point of view of the media, the truth is the victory of one (truth) over others. Are the media producing the only viable truth?

In the East Village, where I was living for the time being, I found a shoe repair place. A plump little woman was there with the swarthy proprietor. There was a cassette of Russian pop music playing. So I explained in Russian: "The heels need replacing, they need gluing here."

"Where are you from?" asked the cobbler.

"Yugoslavia."

"Ah," they sighed compassionately, nodding.

"Come back in an hour. I'll fix them right away," said the cobbler warmly, taking my shoes.

"Good luck," said the little woman with her strong accent, nodding in compassion. Something caught in my throat, I suddenly felt like crying, because of that momentary understanding, because of the sudden burst of brotherly warmth, because of the raw nakedness of the whole situation.

"Okay, okay," I muttered almost to myself, hurrying out of the shop.

I called my mother in Zagreb.

"It's just the same as when you left . . . They're shelling Dubrovnik again. Vukovar has been demolished, they're shelling Osijek, Karlovac . . . I don't know how we'll get by. They're throwing this 'cobweb' thing over us. No, don't worry, they say it isn't poisonous. We're fine. We've just come up from the shelter. What worries me most is that you left without your winter coat. Is it cold there already? They've started running the heat here, but only sporadically. We're out of natural gas, they say. Who knows how we'll manage this winter. So do they know about us there? Are they writing about us? Don't worry. For the time being we're safe and sound."

I shatter into little pieces, I feel I'll never pull myself back together again. It makes no difference at all whether I'm here or there, the fear is just as powerful, horror wraps itself around me like a cobweb. And I wonder which is real: all that came before or now this, after? I wonder where this appalling evil came from, this cruelty, this mindless destruction. What is this dreadful need to destroy everything that was built up, to burn it, raze it to the ground, where does it come from? What is this urge to kill for the sake of killing, without reason or aim, where does it come from? Which one is, indeed, real: all that came before or now this, after?

When she heard I was a writer, a young New Yorker interested in "Eastern Europe" asked, "So how are things now, after perestroika, I mean censorship and all that?"
"I'm sorry, but you've got the wrong country," I said.
"Oh yes, excuse me," she apologized hastily. "You're the country where there's a war on, right?"
"Yes, we're the country where there's a war on."
"Sorry," she said, well-meaning, smiling.

A gray November morning. I went out for a walk along St. Mark's Place. Pressed up against the houses there were homeless people asleep; others were wriggling out of their tattered bedding and lighting their first morning cigarettes. It was still early for New York, it wasn't yet ten o'clock. The street was deserted, the trinket sellers hadn't yet set out their stalls.

Suddenly I felt an irresistible urge to sit down here on the street for a while, to wrap myself in tatters like the homeless, to lean against the wall of a building, to crawl into a cardboard box.

Lit by the gray morning light, a man was walking toward me. He stretched out his arms, flapping them like wings, a black angel. For a moment his eyes met mine.

"Good morning, America!" he shouted at the top of his lungs, his face wreathed in smiles.

All at once I flapped my arms too, about to take off.

"Good morning," I said.

The Organizer

1. "ORGANIZER" WAS the first word I stumbled across and I've been tripping over it ever since. I don't know whether it adopted me, or I it, this word, this thing, *the organizer.*

2. When I go into American supermarkets I don't look around, I head straight for the back of the vast space crammed with merchandise, I go to find them—the organizers. The organizers glisten with a cold plastic sheen. Organizers for socks (each pair in its own plastic berth), organizers for dresses, organizers for shoes, for ties, for jewelry, organizers for sweaters, folding ones with little cardboard shelves, big ones for coats. Organizers of fiberboard in various colors, to be assembled to make drawers, little cupboards, little wardrobes, shelves . . . Special hanging organizers, so special, so collapsible, so practical, bring order to cupboards gone awry. Organizers for business cards (each in its own plastic slot), organizers for pencils, for addresses and telephone numbers, for checks and money, for manuscripts, documents, files, for every article, every purpose, every occasion.

3. When I write, I number every section. This is how I organize my thoughts. Numbers seem to be the most accurate symbol of the organizer.

4. America is an organized country. Organizers are cast across American everyday life like a fine-meshed net. Organizers greet the traveler who arrives in America. At the airport, passengers wait for passport control organized neatly into lines by snaking cordons. Americans lined up one behind the other (like those business cards stacked in their organizer) enter their own country in an organized sequence. The *others*, the ones who are not Americans, enter in another. Snaking cordons organize by winding and twisting through banks, post offices. Snakelike ropes channel the waiting person's journey.

In America you can buy pizza in an organized way as well, if you happen, of course, to like pizza. Which I do. The organizer-person calls numbers out over a microphone. I hold a slip of paper with the number I was given earlier and wait impatiently for my turn. When I hear my number, I hurry to take my organized pizza, identified by number. It's tastier that way.

Americans are not afraid of numbers. Except the number 13. This is why the only day when you can, without difficulty, find flight tickets on the busier routes is the thirteenth of the month. This is why high-rise buildings often have no thirteenth floor.

5. Americans walk like organizers. During lunchtime in New York, armies of organized people swarm out of their offices. Men in white shirts, suits, ties, neatly shaven and groomed, women in suits with high-heeled shoes and trim hairstyles. Many people perform the business of lunch with lunch boxes, soda cans neatly dressed in brown paper bags, sitting or standing, tidily discarding the leftovers in

trash cans. Only a few show an absence of organization: the ones who smoke, leaning against the walls of the skyscrapers. They have descended to Earth from their celestial office-organizers and are blowing little smoke rings of chaos into the air. That's how it is on Wall Street. In the organizer that is Manhattan, chaos lies between C and D Avenues, in Harlem, and elsewhere. At the center is order, chaos is on the edges.

6. The organizer is the only viable weapon in the battle against chaos. An innocent hanger-organizer vanquishes chaos as effectively as a menacing machete. Because it, chaos, can only be a threat to societies that are organized.

7. Chaos squints through a teensy hole in a tooth (call the dentist!), it insinuates itself into neglected nails (call the pedicurist!), peers through the dark roots of dyed hair (to the hairdresser, quick!), chaos seeps through a stain on clothing (to the local laundry!), it ogles through the hole in a sock, threatens on all sides, chaos knocks at the door with unpaid bills, with the prospect of job loss, of serious illness, chaos lurks in the cardboard box that is home to the homeless, it drips off fat passersby, grins from the faces of addicts, chaos rises in vapor from sewer shafts, yawns from the gutted, charred houses in the Bronx, at night it scuttles through trash cans, chaos cackles, oozes out of dark holes, fat, terrible, and black as a city rat.

8. That is why people invented organizers. Chaos is divvied up into little piles, stowed away in shiny plastic compartments and closed with a zip-lock. Zip! There. No more chaos. No more darkness.

9. I am fond of organizers. I buy them wherever I can. My room is filling up with them. Clothes-organizers, desk-organizers . . . I haven't yet taken any action. I'm just a newcomer to the purchasing

of organizers. Their cold plastic sheen glistens. They soothe me. They are a substitute for my lost home, one day I'll stow my own chaos away in them.

10. I don't know where my former home is or where my future home will be, I don't know whether I have a roof over my head, I don't know what to think of my childhood, my origins, my languages. What about my Croatian, my Serbian, my Slovene, my Macedonian? What about the hammer and the sickle, my old coat of arms and my new one, or the yellow star? What to do with the dead, with the living, with the past or the future. I'm walking, talking chaos. This is why I buy organizers.

11. In the weekly news magazine, *Vreme* (which I buy regularly on 42nd Street), I read news from my homeland. In Vukovar, having first destroyed the city and its people, the Federal Army soldiers steal pony-bikes from local department stores. Every soldier, every "victor," tows behind him a child's bicycle. On their soldiers' helmets are stenciled in Cyrillic the ominous words: *Silent Liquidation Detachments.* Organizers. Kill—cleanse—organize. The situation in Vukovar is truly appalling. People, soldiers, the occasional journalist. A soldier doles out water, canned food, and bread.

"How are you doing now that it's over?" a journalist asks a woman.

"Over?" says the woman. "Our house is in ruins, we have nothing left, we don't know where they're taking us, they shelled and bombed us so badly that we've lost our compass. We're no longer sane. What exactly do you see as being 'over'?" fumes the woman in a rage.

The soldier offers her a bottle of soda. "Get lost, you and your bottle!" says the woman.

A young man turns to the soldier: "What use is a bottle when you've taken all our openers?"

I close the magazine. O—opener. O—order. O—organizer. Where can I stow my anguish and my despair?

12. My shoes-organizer has twelve pockets. All my organizers have an even number of compartments. I'm aware of the importance of organization. I'll never be like my American acquaintance, Judith, who lives alone in a ramshackle house ruled by two immense cats, while she forever dreams of moving to Greece. No, I'll never be like the Croatian poet, V., who was finally ousted, after many years, from her apartment by mountains of menacing, disorganized rubbish. No, I'll also not be like my crazy Moscow friend Zhenya who crammed his apartment so full of aquariums that in the end he crashed, with his entire watery menagerie and home (ah, Soviet incompetence!), into the apartment below. And no, I don't want to be like my American friend Norman who swore he wouldn't clean his apartment until he'd sorted through his tax documents, and that was months ago. I won't be like them. They're done for. I'll be my very own office for the silent liquidation of chaos, I'll organize myself. I'll be American. I'll stop smoking. One day I'll be cold, shiny, slippery, and completely plastic. Like an organizer.

Missing

My mother collects other people's deaths, rattling them mournfully like coins in a piggy bank.

"Did you know Petrović died?" asks Mother over the phone.

"Really?" I say, although I have no idea who this Petrović is.

"Yes, imagine, a *heart attack*," says Mother, stressing the words.

"Oh," I say.

"Poor man," sighs Mother, ending her little verbal funeral rite. And she files Petrović away in her mental piggy-bank.

Mother tells me these sorts of things. Talking about them allows her to prolong anonymous Petrović's life for another moment, light him an invisible candle; by counting out other people's deaths like pocket change she holds her own fears at bay.

But I'm not interested in deaths. They are so final. I'm interested in disappearances.

One year my Zagreb friend Knaflec disappeared as well. People said he'd gone to America. When I first went to America, someone gave me his phone number. I called the number, somewhere in Texas. He answered, but the person I was speaking to was no longer my friend Knaflec. Now I don't think of calling him—he too has disappeared.

And then one year there was a journalist who took up my favorite theme of disappearance and wrote an article about it. It turned out that 2,847 people had disappeared in Yugoslavia that year. I even remember the exact figure. That year, 2,847 Yugoslavs could not be found among the living or the dead.

I find New York the most confusing. As I walk through the city's streets I often think I must be in the middle of a nightmare. I see a man with a plastic bag. There's a long stick of American celery poking from it. And I can clearly see: he's my friend Nenad. "Hey, Nenad," I call. "Hey, what are you doing here?" He looks at me but doesn't recognize me. Goodness, I whisper, confused. He shrugs his shoulders and walks on with the long stick of celery in his bag.

A taxi passes. In it is my friend Berti. "Hey, Berti!" The taxi stops at a crossing, the light's red. "Hey, Berti!" Berti looks at me through the window, he smiles but he doesn't recognize me. What's this, I think, if he were here, if that were Berti, he'd surely say hello, I think. But I'm not certain.

At the park I watch a cleaner clearing away dry leaves. He blows them away with an enormous leaf blower, making rustling, golden-yellow heaps. A magician. For a moment I clearly see the profile of my friend Pavle. "Hey, Pavle, how come you're here?" I shout. "Hey!" I go up to him and tap him on the shoulder. He turns around and says, in English, with no foreign accent: "Stop that, ma'am, or I'll call the police."

So I give up. The newspaper seller on the corner is my Zagreb friend, Vilma. I buy the papers from her every day on the corner of Eighth

Street and University Place. I gaze at her for a long time, put the money into her hand knowingly and take my *New York Times.* I don't say a word, I'm no longer insisting, I pretend I don't know she's Vilma. "Thank you, have a nice day."

Here in Middletown the situation is altogether different. It's a small town, I don't know a soul, I'm a stranger, they're at home, locals. But still, to be on the safe side, I memorize every face. The salesperson at Bob's, the cashier at Waldbaum's, the waiter at the Opera House, the cop by the Clock Tower. I let my eyes range over the names in the local telephone directory. Brigith, Gloria; Kilby, Peter; Hills, Karen . . . I don't know anyone. I feel safe and serene. Everything is as it should be. I'm a stranger, they are locals, at home.

At about noon each day the mailman comes and brings the mail. I open the Zagreb newspapers of November 29, 1991. I read an article about missing persons. Thirty thousand missing persons have been registered in Croatia, writes the author. People are looking for their vanished brothers, husbands, wives, children, parents. Not only have several villages and towns been razed to the ground, but these 30,000 people are gone as well. They can no longer be found among the living or the dead.

Terrible, I think. It's just as well that I'm here where it's safe. I'm a stranger here, they're all at home, everything is as it should be. Someone called Peter lives near me, someone called Gloria, someone called Karen. I'm protected, nothing can happen to me.

Suddenly I hear the doorbell, I go to the door, open it—and people I have never seen before surge into my apartment. They pour in uncontrollably like a flood, women, children, old men, the wounded, soldiers. "I'm Željko," a young man introduces himself, "it's two months since I went missing somewhere near Pirot, my sister Ljubica Oreški is

looking for me." "I'm a mother," mumbles a woman, "I disappeared in September, somewhere near Drniš; my son, Rade Brakus, is looking for me."
And I understand, here they are, all 30,000. "Come in," I say, "find somewhere to sit, make yourselves at home, we'll manage somehow." They arrange themselves quietly. There are so many, I think, and they all fit into my small apartment, as if they were transparent, I think, as if they were playing cards, one laid down over the other. That's because they've disappeared, I think, that's why they're so collapsible.

And as I cook a meal to feed them all, I think about how the globe is like an egg timer, like communicating vessels, there's a copy of everything, as in a library. There's a Berlin here in my neighborhood, ten minutes' drive away, West and East, nothing has been left out. There's a copy of everything somewhere, especially here, there's a Paris in Texas, and a Moscow and a Madrid and a Copenhagen and a Venice and a London and a Hamburg, and New York is merely another name for New Amsterdam . . . The missing don't disappear, then, they simply spring up elsewhere, for instance in my apartment. It's all right, I think, everything's all right, there's no need to worry, I'll look after your brother, Ljubica Oreški.

The telephone rings, it's my mother calling from Zagreb.
"Did you know . . ." she begins slowly and I already anticipate the familiar, soft rattle in the receiver.
"I know, Mother, no need to tell me. They're here, we all are," I say, and I hear a rich jangle like a slot machine suddenly spitting out a whole pile of coins.

Manual

"I'm madly in love . . . But, it's Madeline . . . she doesn't want me," complains my American friend, Norman.

"Oh?" I say.

"So I'm off to Croatia to die," says this infatuated doctor of political science who once spent a year in Zagreb on a Fulbright.

"Why Croatia? You're not even from there."

"I figured I'd kill myself anyway, for Madeline. Better to die romantically."

"If you have to kill yourself, best do it practically," I say, adding: "There's a handbook for that sort of thing."

"A manual?"

Manuals are the American bible. American everyday life is a culture of manuals. Sacred directions or instructions, they're like the informative little square of cloth that comes inscribed with a mass of words you'll find attached to a small plush teddy bear, a child's toy. Everything is written on the label: the material the bear's made of and what you should and shouldn't do with it, not in the mouth, not near an open flame, not this and not that. With instructions for its use, the little plush bear becomes a serious thing.

Americans shop as though they were taking an important exam. Buying ordinary tennis shoes can take an hour. Americans establish a kind of oral manual with the salesman. What are the laces made of, can you easily wiggle your toes, what about the tongue, and the sole, and how flexible are they, and what are they made of, and what's the lining like, and what's the difference between these and those. The assistant offers the instructions as if he were an orthopedic surgeon and not an ordinary salesman. The American consumer listens and speaks as though he were a patient rather than an ordinary customer.

At the entrance to vast American supermarkets, the buyer is met by an array of free brochures. Enough for a whole newspaper stand. Just buying bread, a person can learn something about radon, radioactive gas, the new bogeyman of American daily life; as he buys cornflakes he can learn something about panic disorder, about symptoms that until a moment before he had romantically believed were a sign of sudden anxiety or metaphysical dread (I always went for the latter, myself), and now, it turns out that it's ordinary, surmountable fear. As he buys his Thanksgiving turkey, a person may inform himself about how to pay less income tax; as he buys sparkling water, he may obtain free advice on bedwetting, which (bedwetting that is) may cause serious problems later in life: it may undermine one's self-image, or damage one's self-esteem. As he buys sausages, a person may learn how to get rich quick or buy a house; as he selects a boneless joint, he can take a free booklet, *The Dating Page,* and discover how to find a suitable partner for a life à deux.

And while I, a foreigner, am consumed by a panic disorder because I don't know what to do with the booklet full of coupons guaranteeing me *big savings*—I can't decide whether I want a boneless joint for only $3.59 or a male, healthy, handsome companion, a nonsmoker who enjoys dancing, skiing, sailing, parachuting, and romantic candlelit dinners. I don't know whether I should get rich first so I can afford the boneless joint for only $3.59, or buy the boneless joint and then find my lifelong companion later—meanwhile ordinary Americans swim through it all like fish in water. They are used to a system that leads them to their desired objective, like a video game.

But in order to accomplish this you must first master the instructions. Intuition is useless here, and besides, intuition is for the chosen few, while the equitable American system offers you what is attainable for everyone. Manuals, instructions, handbooks. You have to read, read carefully, read right through without skipping. Besides, wherever the reader's attention begins to flag you find large letters proclaiming Keep Reading! You have to keep on reading, no interruptions, not missing anything (Don't Miss This!). There is nothing in the world that cannot be mastered with the aid of clear instructions.

The culture of manuals that leads you to your desired aim is effective because it is based on a deeply mythical premise: the archetype of the labyrinth. It is a future and bygone fairy tale about Ivan the Fool, who reaches his desired goal by overcoming all obstacles, following strict instructions (strict!). And his goal, of course, is a kingdom and a glamorous princess! Those who sin, dissidents who defy the system, those who, like Pandora, open the box despite the instructions to the contrary, such people mean trouble for both themselves and the world. The video game is therefore a modern fairy tale: the culture of the manual has its hero, its video-game player, its Ivan the Fool. Whoever follows the instructions must reach the desired goal. No one can shake the American's fundamental belief in this conviction. *Keep reading! Keep living!*

And what if he doesn't? What if he doesn't reach the desired goal despite the instructions? asks my skeptical, my suspicious, my cynical, my lazy, my ironic, my destructive mind. And what if he doesn't?

And I can see myself already, I know, I give up from the start: I'll never be rich, I'll never have a beautiful house and a lifelong companion keen on sailing, skiing, flying, and what's more a nonsmoker, I'll never get my tax rebate, I'll never lose all those extra pounds, I'll never get my body into satisfactory shape, I'll never buy a boneless joint for only $3.59, I'll never stop smoking, I'll never win the lottery, I won't, not ever . . .

I'm not master of myself, I'm not master of anything. When I probe the depths of my dissidence, when I reach the very last "I won't" or "I can't," there's still a chance for me! America has taken this into account. *Final Exit. The Manual.* A handbook for suicide, or in a loftier lingo—for self-deliverance. I'll read the final instructions carefully, slowly, no rush. I'll choose my final exit like a gourmet dish at the toniest restaurant. I'll run my eyes slowly over the menu: *Death Hollywood-Style*, *Bizarre Ways to Die*, *Self-Deliverance via Plastic Bag.* I'll buy myself a little calculator so I can convert the ounces to grams, I'll learn everything, I'll study everything, I'll be a perfectionist.

In the world of manuals everything is easy, painless, and safe. Nevertheless I trust in Unpredictability as the Great Poetic Idea. Because perhaps on the screen of the new interactive computers, in those new manuals, where an ordinary finger has the power of a magic wand, perhaps by touching a little astral circle on the screen I'll be able to open a passageway, a door, and perhaps, like Alice, I'll slip through a tunnel into another world, a world on the other side of the Manual.

The phone rings, it's my American friend Norman.

"Madeline loves me, she said so today," he announces cheerfully.

"Oh?" I say.

"It was silly of me to say I'd kill myself. Madeline wants me. Did you hear?"

"I did."

"So why are you sad?"

"Dubrovnik has been shelled."

"Oh? I'm sorry, I really am," he says, genuinely upset. We say nothing for a time, and then my American friend asks cautiously, "What do you think, did Madeline really mean it when she said she loved me?"

Shrink

For some time now I've had a shrink. No American with a smidgen of self-respect knows who he or she is: that's why every American has a shrink. And, although I'm a foreigner, I do have self-respect and I don't know who I am. My shrink is a woman, a bleached blonde who looks a lot like the star of my childhood, Doris Day.

"You see, there was a bad earthquake in Montenegro a few years ago. Afterward a journalist asked a shepherd what it had been like. 'Well,' said the shepherd, 'I was in my house when I felt something shake. I went outside and saw it: the epicenter! I ran to the left, but the epicenter came after me, I ran to the right, and the epicenter came after me again.'"

"Amusing," says my shrink with a faint smile.

"It's not amusing," I say. "That's why I've come to you. You see, the epicenter is after me. The ground is trembling underfoot, I keep seeing double, I'm feeling everything is so fragile that it'll shatter any

minute." I speak like an intelligent person who expresses herself in metaphors and doesn't tax her listeners with the details.
"Please don't express yourself in metaphors, be concrete. To begin with, please elaborate. What is Montenegro?" asks my shrink pointedly.

So I explain. Why not. In the general melee it's absolutely immaterial where to start. I list them all: Montenegro and Slovenia, Croatia, Bosnia and Herzegovina, Macedonia and Serbia. I also mention the two former autonomous provinces, Vojvodina and Kosovo.
"Why former?" asks the shrink.
I explain that too. And I list them: Slovenes and Croats, Serbs and Muslims, Montenegrins and Albanians, Jews and Italians, Gypsies and Romanians, Bulgarians and Romanians, Hungarians and Czechs . . . I list them all, I leave nothing out.
"Keep it brief, please, so we can get on to the fundamental source of your frustration," says my shrink.
"I did start with the epicenter, but you asked me to explain Montenegro," I say, indignant.
"Sure, sure," mumbles my shrink. "Do go on."

So I do, I explain the history of Yugoslavia and my own personal history along the way, I dust off my grandmothers and grandfathers, not for my sake, but, I think, maybe she, the shrink, needs to know, I recall my own childhood, I leave nothing out, not my pioneer neckerchief, or the work brigades, or Tito's relay race.
"Wait, what. What about that Tito relay race thing?"

So I explain. A tube of wood or tin, a hollow baton, handmade, and for years some 22 million Yugoslavs stuffed little scraps of paper into ones like it—messages for Tito's birthday, symbolically passing the baton from hand to hand like a pledge to brotherhood and unity.

"I don't quite understand, but it's obviously phallic," says my shrink professionally.
"Of course," I say. "I come from a phallic culture, male; a culture of batons, truncheons, and knives, as needed. Let's skip that for now, it's getting us nowhere."
"But obviously that's what brought you to where you are now," she observes acidly.
"Well you slurped Coca-Cola and twirled those 'pompoms' around when you were a cheerleader at school, yet you seem to be doing okay," I say boldly.
"So I did. I'd almost forgotten," murmurs my Doris Day with a pang. "Do continue."

So I do. I leave nothing out. I tell her about socialism, about our mindset, collectivism, about the collective *we* instead of the individual *I*, about the *we* who is never responsible, in whose name a bright future was always promised, in whose name people are now slaughtering each other . . .

"I see. If you'd had a more developed sense of the 'self' everything would be so much better for you now."
"Then we'd have individual instead of collective lunacy."
"Explain."

So I explain. I presented her with a brief history of our debacle. I talk about mythic, tribal thinking, about primitive savagery, illiteracy, the criminal mentality, about theft, lies, the legitimation of lies, about the culture of lies, the pigheadedness, the new-fangled rural psyche that weeps as it murders and murders as it weeps . . .
"Give me something more concrete. I don't understand a thing you're saying."

So I explain. I enumerate dates, names, I give the results of the democratic elections in percentages, I list the parties in power and those in opposition, I list the names of leaders, events, cities.
"Milosevik . . . Vu-ko-var." The shrink struggles with the names.

And on I go. I talk about the savagery of the army, about Serbian and Montenegrin weekend warriors plundering Dubrovnik, the collective paranoia, the lies, about the devastated Croatian towns, the murdered children, the torched villages, about the massacres, the refugees, the drunkenness, about the madness, the cult of the knife.

And I notice my shrink's hands trembling slightly.
"Enough. It sounds like you're retelling horror movies. I doubt any of this can be happening in the middle of Europe, on the verge of the twenty-first century," says my shrink in a schoolmarmy tone. "So tell me, what is your problem?" she continues sternly.
"My problem is that this is all true, this is no horror movie."
"Talk to me about your personal problems," she says, stressing *personal,* as though all the above doesn't come under the rubric of the personal.

So I gladly go on explaining. I am a split personality, I'm seeing double, I'm housing parallel worlds, everything is going on simultaneously in my head. I look at the American flag and suddenly it seems as if I'm seeing miniature red sickles and hammers instead of the white stars. I watch an ad for necklaces, those are the ones I find the most soothing, but instead of a pearl necklace for a mere 65 dollars I see a slashed throat. I walk down Fifth Avenue and suddenly see the buildings toppling like houses of cards. Everything is blurring in my mind, it is all going on at once, nothing has just one meaning any more, nothing feels steadfast, not the ground beneath my feet, nor the national borders, people, houses . . . Everything is so fragile it feels about to shatter at any minute.

"And worst of all," I say in anguish, "I feel it's all my fault, that I'm carrying the virus. At the moment I'm the most worried about the Empire State Building and the Brooklyn Bridge."
"Nothing can happen to you. You're safe here," says my shrink with conviction.
"I was safe there, too, but then this happened."
"You're in a state of shock, that's all, everything will be fine."
"But what about the virus? What if at this very moment, while the two of us are talking, the Empire State Building is tumbling down! And you say everything will be fine!"
"You yourself know that's impossible!"
"That's what I thought about Dubrovnik!"
"Jesus Christ, this really is too much! Work on your self-esteem, which is seriously damaged. I'll see you a week from Friday," says my Doris Day bringing the session resolutely to a close. Her hands are still trembling slightly and she looks paler than she did at the beginning.

And I take her advice. I do yoga every day, I work on myself, on my well-being. I am the center of the world, nothing else interests me, nothing else exists, and no one can divert me from my path. I gaze at my outstretched leg like it's an object worthy of respect, I don't think about anything, I listen to music, the best stress buster, new age, and I've ordered a brain supercharger, I'm expecting it any day now. I've forgotten all about my shrink, as though I'd never been to see her.

The telephone rings. I don't pick up. I'm used to this too. I sit in a lotus pose, I don't stir. I'm beginning to see the results of this work on myself. It doesn't occur to me to move or answer the phone. A familiar voice pours out of the answering machine.

"Hello? What's wrong? Hello? Where are you? Why don't you pick up? Please, call me. I need your help. It's here in my clinic. The epicenter! I'm at a loss. Everything's shaking, I'm seeing double, everything is so fragile it feels about to shatter at any minute . . ."

Jogging

"It's terrible. Madeline's left me again. She's gone off with this other guy. I can't go on. I've had it," Norman moans in Croatian. His despair surges over the phone, splashing my sensitive ear like warm wax.

"Everything will be fine," I say.

"It will not," is all he responds.

"Cheer up!" I say and realize at once that I've struck a wrong note. You should never offer words of consolation in a language other than your own.

"Please tell me, for God's sake, what's happening," says my friend in a voice which sends uncomfortable shivers down my spine (and this is me, the expert in Russian literature)!

"It's all as simple as strawberry jam, Norman," I say. "You're head-over-heels. And your Madeline's only throwing grease on the fire with her 'now I do, now I don't' attitude."

"No," sighs Norman into the receiver. "It's not that simple, it's all so much more complicated . . ." and after a long pause he adds in a bleak voice, "Maybe I'm feeling so awful because I haven't been jogging in a week."

There are white plastic blinds on the windows of my apartment. In the morning as soon as I get up I go straight to the window. I part the blinds a little, let a horizontal shaft of light into the room, and lean my forehead against the cool plastic. Secretly I peer through the horizontal gaps. I wait. Gazing out at the empty sports field like this extends my warm drowsiness a little longer. And there he is, he's coming, my solitary jogger. His red hair tied in a ponytail, his marble-white face, hidden gaze, he runs rhythmically and effortlessly. I can see it's cold outside by the steam he exhales. One-two, one-two, my lonely jogger runs, my jo-gg-er, morning light of my life. My sweet voyeuristic sin, jo-gg-errrr . . . Jo-gg-errr: the tip of my tongue trips down my palate and then suddenly flips up like a little snake and slides back down my throat.

The jogger goes out of sight, I can't see him anymore but I know: he'll come this way again tomorrow. "Jogger!" I expel the guttural sound. In the quiet emptiness of my room the word rings softly like a mother-of-pearl Chinese rattle.

The weather in Connecticut is capricious. The bright winter sun makes the right angles of the town streets even sharper, more regular. Light and shadow alternate as if on a chessboard. The chess pieces have names like: *Waldbaum's*, *Caldor*, *Sears*, *Stop & Shop* . . . On those sunny days a gust of cold wind buffets your face unexpectedly, darting out of ambush and dipping around the corner. On Main Street is the Clock Tower with an enormous clock on top. A policeman patrols under the tower. The hands on the clock are long, black, and sharp like the shadow cast by the policeman's truncheon. The clock and the policeman harmonize the rhythm of the day.

At night I often wake, disturbed by the ticking of an inner clock. I rise, go to the window, slowly part the blinds and stare into the dark. I often feel he is here, my jogger. He stops, looks at me, tilts his head to the side, and waits. In the darkness I imagine his thighs damp with sweat, I feel his steady pulse, the warmth of his breath. Wrapped in emptiness like a blanket, I stare into the dark.

Every day I buy something. In secret. I pretend at the store that I'm shopping for my brother, my husband, my friend, "Just the thing for my nephew," I say, "those headbands, you know, the kind athletes wear . . ." "Aha, a sweatband," says the long-suffering salesman and brings me the band I'm after. I learn the words, I buy the things to teach myself the words, I learn the words so I can buy the things. *Jog-a-lites* are reflective gear, colored stick-ons, bands for runners who run in the dark.

Every day I buy something. I arrange the purchases in my room as if I'm a bride admiring her wedding dress, I study them, handle them, but I still don't dare wear any of them. I don't tell anyone about my passion, I shop in secret, I tote the booty to my lair.

One-two, one-two, runs my lonely jogger. I make out his thighs, moist with sweat, the drops of sweat on his upper lip. The capricious Connecticut wind buffets his pale face. One-two, one-two, runs my lonely jogger.

The legs, so delicately shaped, balanced a
body wrought of finest ivory. And as
he moved, his coat shone like reflected moonlight.
High on his forehead rose the magic horn, the sign
of his uniqueness: a tower held upright
by his alert, yet gentle, timid gait.

The mouth of softest tints of rose and grey, when
opened slightly, revealed his gleaming teeth,
whiter than snow. The nostrils quivered faintly:
he sought to quench his thirst, to rest and find repose.
His eyes looked far beyond the saint's enclosure,
reflecting vistas and events long vanished,
*and closed the circle of this ancient mystic legend.**

Running shoes: $78.99; sweatsuit: $73.29; sweatsocks: $5.99; sweat-shirt: $12.99; sweatpants: $19.00; gym shorts: $17.99; sweatband: $5.99; T-shirt: $10.50 . . .

At night I often wake, disturbed by the ticking of an inner clock. I rise, go to the window, slowly part the blinds and let horizontal shafts of moonlight fall into the room. I stare long into the dark. And then without switching on the light I don my new, clean T-shirt, my snow-white cotton socks, my warm new cotton sweatsuit, over that I put on a light nylon windbreaker then I take my new white running shoes, try them on carefully like a samurai testing the blade of his sword. Over my brow, as if it were a wedding garland, I pull on a brightly colored sweatband.

I go to the window, stare into the dark and wait patiently. First I see two bright yellow fluorescent spots. The yellow spots chase each other through the night and then abruptly disappear. He's standing outside my window lit by the moonlight, looking at me with his head tilted to one side, waiting. I go out, the capricious Connecticut wind buffets my face. I go up to him, touch his red hair, run my hand over his face. "My jogger," I whisper, my sweet voyeuristic sin. He holds out his hand without a word, pulls me along and we start to run in the

* Rainer Maria Rilke, "The Unicorn," translated by Albert Ernest Flemming.

dark. One-two, one-two . . . Suddenly I feel we're weightless, rising skyward, we're tracing the paths marked by the streetlights. Solitary letters shine in the dark like big stars: *Waldbaum's*, *Caldor*, *Stop & Shop*, *Sears* . . . One-two, one-two, we run easily, silently, as if over cotton batting. The clock on the Clock Tower is as round and bright as the full moon. We run above Main Street, turn into Court Street, we run above High Street . . . One-two, one-two, my jogger, rhythm of my breath, jogger, rhythm of my heart, jogger, fire of my loins, jogger, jogger, jogger . . . Keep on repeating this word, typesetter, to the bottom of the page . . .

Homeland

"SHE BROUGHT ME the mouse," says Beka, pointing in my direction.

"How could I have 'brought' it?" I protest.

"The mouse showed up when you did."

"Maybe it was here before but you didn't notice," says the actress soothingly.

"I'd have noticed," says Beka.

"How'd it come in?" asks the filmmaker.

"Through the air vents, they come in through the air vents around here," says the archeologist.

"In any case, there were never any mice here before," says Beka, shaking her head.

"New York is teeming with mice, it's perfectly natural for one to turn up at your place," says the journalist. "All large cities are full of mice. Amsterdam, for instance, one day it'll be overrun."

"And Paris."

"And Berlin."

"I don't give a damn about Berlin! Everything was fine in my apartment until she came," says Beka, pointing my way.

We are sitting in Beka's apartment, the lights of New York are sparkling through the window, we chat, jabber, shift the words around our mouths like nuts, taking care not to bite into the kernel. All of us just "happened" to be here. Some of us are teaching at American universities for a semester or two, some have scholarships, some are passing through, more or less like tourists. An actress, an elder filmmaker, a younger filmmaker, a psychologist, a journalist, a writer, an archeologist . . . All from more or less the same branch, all more or less the same age (forty or so), all out of more or less the same social, intellectual, and ideological kindergarten.

We study each other, we feel both awkwardness and pity, as we would for members of our own family. Because once (oh, so long ago) we all wore a pioneer neckerchief, we all waved flags to greet visitors with unpronounceable names (*Nkrumah*, *Sirimavo Bandaranaike*, *Haile Selassie*), we all learned our letters from the same primer (H—for homeland), and sentences from the same reader (*Tito says: Cherish brotherhood and unity, your most precious gift*) . . . Oh, when was that! And can it really have been our own, shared history, or was it just a movie in which we were child extras? And then we grew up and forgot it all. And then off we scattered through our own lives. We popped off on a jaunt to Trieste, to London, to Paris, a jaunt to New York, but it didn't actually occur to anyone to move away, why should we, why would any of us have actually wanted to move away, life was good, skiing in winter in the Slovenian mountains, summer by the sea. The Adriatic.

No, no one moved away. Nothing, actually, ever happened.

For a moment in Beka's apartment we stopped, for a moment we all mused to ourselves about how it was that we weren't socializing in a Zagreb, Sarajevo, or Belgrade cafe, but instead were here, in New York, and how it was that there were suddenly so many of us, and we all knew each other, what a fluke, and how it was that we were all, more or less, the same age . . .

No, no one moved away. And nothing actually ever happened. Except perhaps to the actress. She'd been declared a traitor. By both sides. The West and the East. Actress-traitor! Actress-traitor!

"Don't take it personally," we say to the actress. Some have been killed, others have fled, some have lost the roof over their heads, others their career, some are dead, others still alive, no one is unscathed.

No, no one moved away. And nothing actually ever happened. Except perhaps to the younger filmmaker. Once, twenty years earlier, he made a movie. And he was put in prison. He came out of prison and left the country. Then went back. Now he has left again. He couldn't stand the same old story.
"I'm fifty already," says the elder filmmaker.
"Don't take it personally," we say to the elder filmmaker. Some have been killed, others have fled, some have lost the roof over their heads, others their career, no one is unscathed.

"I'll get a job as a waiter," says the younger filmmaker. "How could I direct anything here? There are thousands like me. I feel like a penguin at the North Pole."
"South Pole," says Beka.
"Why?"
"Because penguins live at the South Pole."

"And I'll sell discarded scrap from the proverbial communist dustbin," says the journalist. "I'll give them the image of the world they expect, the stereotypes of life behind 'the Iron Curtain,' the stereotypes of a gray, alienated Eastern Europe standing in line for sauerkraut."

"But we never stood in line for sauerkraut," we protest.

"So what. *They* think we did and that's what matters. I'll sell our Yugo-souvenirs as well, our sickle, hammer, knife. Tomorrow it'll be too late, tomorrow the whole world will have swept it under the rug anyway," says the journalist.

"I simply can't go back. It all makes me sick," says the actress.

No, no one moved away . . .

"The last chunk of the Berlin Wall has been sold. Lenin's cap and Stalin's moustache have been sold," says the psychologist, shaking his head.

"Why's that? What do Lenin's cap and Stalin's moustache have to do with all of us?" asks Beka.

"I'll get a job as a waiter. What else can I do? Show my movies around American universities for a hundred dollars a gig? There's a recession on here, too. We came at the wrong time."

No, no one moved away. And nothing, actually, ever happened.

"Whenever we came here it would have been the wrong time," says the writer.

"We didn't change gears on time, we're has-beens. Now there are other actresses, other filmmakers, other journalists, other writers . . . back home," says the psychologist.

"What home?" asks Beka.

"It all happened too fast. I refused to participate, and I refused because

I was disgusted, because I was afraid . . . who cares. No one will be asking why anymore," says the elder filmmaker.
"I suddenly feel just like the Russian émigrés in Paris or Berlin seventy years ago," says the psychologist.
"They've torn down everything I'd been excavating for twenty years," says the archeologist. "Twenty years! Layer after layer, piece by piece, for twenty years. Now it's all back underground again . . ."
"I simply can't move forward. Recently, I hardly change out of my pajamas. All I want to do is sleep and sleep," says the actress.

"Don't take it personally," we say to the actress. "Some have been killed, others have fled, others have lost the roof over their heads, others their career, some have lost their homeland, others have gained theirs, the only thing that is true is that no one is unscathed."

"I don't want to stay, I don't want to go back, what can I do?" asks one of the filmmakers.
"Do you realize that we are all roughly the same age as Yugoland, the one the cat ate? The mouse the cat ate," says the journalist.

"Hey, want to see it?" asks Beka holding up the dead mouse in an efficient mousetrap.

"Isn't it small!" says the actress, touched.
"Come and dump it into the garbage with me," says Beka.
And we obediently follow Beka into the hallway to the utility room. Beka opens the little flap and drops the mousetrap down the chute. The sound is long and loud, completely out of proportion to the object that caused it.
"There," says Beka, banging shut the little flap.
In a procession, back we file into the apartment. The New York lights

sparkle luxuriously in the windows. New York sparkles like a mouse, like thousands of tiny mice, like thousands of Mickey Mice.

Addict

America has something distinctively hairdresser-like about it. Hair salons are the same the world over. And that's because they aren't, in fact, salons, but a model for human behavior. When I say America has something "hairdresser-like" about it, that is what I have in mind.

As soon as I appear at the door of a hair salon, I am swept into the swirl surrounding the Maestro. The Maestro might be behind a partition mixing dyes, he might have his back to me, he might be circling with his scissors over someone's head, but his gaze, cast like a terrible hook, transforms me into what, in fact, I am: a human being in need of a haircut. There are all sorts of Maestros: friendly, curt, talkative, silent. But the relationship between the Maestro and the customer is always the same—that of master to victim.

It's foolish to expect anything else since your head, one way or another, is in his hands. Whether he follows your instructions, whether he

makes of the coif what I want or what he wants, whether I'll ever show my face in his establishment again, whether I'll give him a tip, none of that matters. He, the Maestro, is the natural master of the situation. And when his job is done, he always asks the same question.
"So, do you like it?"
A question, in other words, which never expects a demurral in salons the world over. Because as a rule it never gets one. This is the law of the genre.
"Yes," I hiss through clenched teeth, though, of course, I do not. This, too, is a rule of the genre. My genre. Because I never go to the hairdresser's to like it, but to dislike it.
However, what makes my displeasure greater than usual, is his, the Maestro's, unshakeable conviction that I *must* like it. And how could I not? I came in with greasy, lackluster hair *(before)* and look at me now *(after)*! My hair is shiny and oh so neatly trimmed!

The Maestro's question—so, do you like it?—reminds me of the question I'm often asked by Americans:
"You'll be staying here, right?"

One of my American nightmares is about entering a store. As soon as I walk in I'm met by the saleswoman's smile.
"How are you today?"
"Fine," I mutter, teeth clenched, then I blush and examine the tips of my shoes.
"How're you doing?"
"Fine," I say again more loudly, and, taking a breath, I raise my eyes to the saleswoman's.

She, poor thing, has no idea that she's already done for. How many have I already slain with that look! Simply because they forced me to utter that innocent little word: fine.

Once, a colleague of mine—one of those who refer to Foucault, Derrida, Lacan, and Baudrillard with the same familiarity as they'd say "Mom," "Dad," and "Grandma"—took me out to eat.
"There are only four restaurants like this in the entire United States," he said as we made our way to the restaurant. "Now at last you'll understand what postmodernism really is."

The restaurant was large and noisy. It was a museum of Americana and everything was there: quotes from American movies and television series, from American history (which we know from the movies and TV series), from American everyday life, American painting (the ones opting for a hyperrealist depiction of everyday life). Everything was there: quote by quote, quote piled upon quote; it was all jumbled together in a vast sort of American salad.

The menu, too, offered undressed quotations: we dutifully ordered our hamburgers and Cokes. Waiters dressed in clown suits entertained the customers with zeal. They'd suddenly flop down across your table while holding the plate and leer into your face as they spun the plate over their head, nearly tipping the contents into your lap. Clown-garbed photographers galumphed about taking pictures of the customers with cheap polaroid cameras and then pressured them to buy the proof of the fun they were having. One group of merrymakers had ordered a huge cake; they flung whipped cream at each other, gamboling like the actors in old comedies.

Pandemonium reigned. This was an aggressive synopsis of American happiness, the image of happiness the American media—movies, series, ads—has been churning out for years, an image of happiness which life itself was now imitating with zeal. The model proved its efficacy for the thousandth time: people were having fun.

A large woman, a sadist done up like a clown, one of the supervisors, was carefully overseeing the level of happiness in the restaurant. At one moment she caught my eye. The Ring Mistress picked up on my inner dismay with the precision of a camera. She immediately pointed at me and summoned the whole room to do the same.
"There, in the corner, that face is not smiling! Yes, take a good look, that woman there, in the black dress . . ." she shrieked into the mic. Then, grinning at me, she playfully wagged her finger. The whole room did the same, savoring the collective reproduction of the gesture. The orchestra struck up "Don't Worry, Be Happy" (what else) and they soon forgot about me. I tugged my postmodernist colleague by the sleeve and out we went. My indoctrinated European brain started to run the familiar images of totalitarian happiness, images of parades, an entire history of happy masses acting the collective body.

"They've imposed a dictatorship of happiness," I stammered weakly.
"It's just a restaurant you can enter and leave as you like," said my colleague, bristling slightly. He was more defensive about American democracy than he was prepared to assuage my sudden surge of dread. And, of course, he was right. It was just a restaurant. And, besides, there were only four like it in the entire United States.
"You'll be staying here, right?" my American acquaintances often ask. The tone of the question never implies the option of a demurral. And what can I say? My hair is, after all, shiny and so neatly trimmed!

My Zagreb acquaintance Ranko M. is a diehard grouch. Whenever we meet, he lets fly lengthy diatribes. Against the state, past, present, and future; against politicians, homegrown and foreign; against his mother who ruined him and his father who was no better; against the legal system, against little kids, though the bigger ones are no better; against dogs and cats, though he finds parakeets as house pets equally vile; against Croats, against Serbs, but also against the French, insufferable, as are the English, the Germans, and the Americans, God knows; against the sun that shines, against the rain that falls, against the planet Earth that is spinning the wrong way, against a universe governed by chaos . . . Nothing you can do will cheer up my Zagreb colleague Ranko M., nothing will console him, that's how he is, a diehard grouch.

Once he stopped by, but this time he miscalculated, he didn't pace his hatred properly, and, after blasting his verbal barrage in all directions, he sputtered to an abrupt finish like a New Year's sparkler. His head slumped to the table and he, my acquaintance, Ranko M., simply stopped. I froze, a heart attack, I thought, and then I heard a reassuring, steady snore. I watched the paroxysm slumber on my table, listened to his contented snores, and thought how varied grousing can be, full of fine, rich nuances.

In this country I am polite. To every "How are you doing?" I reply: "Fine." I no longer even wait to be told, I'm the first to say: "Have a nice day." I have learned the typical cadence as well, the sound that rises brightly like a yodel at the end, a sound that spurs whoever hears it like a dart and infallibly spikes the adrenaline level. Have a nice day, I say to myself, but nothing particular happens. I listen. "Have a nice day," I say again. It echoes dully. I chew on the emptiness like cotton candy, it tastes of nothing. There's something missing, I'm aware of a strange longing, which is, I guess, like that of addiction.

I walk down Main Street and see him, "my" black guy. He's always here, as though he were fused to the road, he's following his lengthy daily route. His eyes are bloodshot, he talks to himself, gesticulates, keeps stopping, raises his fist, threatening someone who can't be seen, a dangerous type.

I walk behind him as though spellbound; I pretend to be going about business of my own. At first I don't understand what he's saying and then I make out the word *fuck.* Daga-da-daga-fuck-daga-da-daga-fucking—he marches like a furious human machine. I walk behind him, I follow the compelling bubbles of loathing he leaves behind.

What more could he want, I think, in a country where you can buy a hamburger for 99 cents, and 99 cents is nearly four quarters, and you can always find four quarters. In phone booths that are out of order you only have to know how, to have the touch . . . Four quarters are a little less than a subway token, and you can always find a token. If nothing else you can suck it out and change it for five quarters, you can suck it out of the metal slot in the subway, as the supple subway rats do, the masters, the master token-suckers, the master mother-fuckers . . .

I often think of my own people standing around on the main Zagreb square, massing like penguins, pounding the pavement for hours, stamping their dissatisfaction into it, bellyaching. Bellyaching against the government, bellyaching against their bad luck, bellyaching because at last they've been recognized, bellyaching because they've not been recognized by the Polynesians . . . These countrymen of mine bellyache, my homebred dejected countrymen, you won't easily coax a smile out of them, they're quite capable of spitting on the street like llamas in response to your *haveaniceday*, that's what my own folk are like, where the streets of life are jammed with traffic accidents, as György Konrád once put it so aptly and sadly.

"You'll be staying here, right?" Americans often ask, unshakeably certain that anything else would be weird. And what else could I do? Haven't I come fresh from "postcommunism"? Haven't I just tossed the "Iron Curtain" into the washing machine? I must have had a rough time of it, poor thing, all that waiting in line for toilet paper; what's more I come from a country where people are brandishing knives over my head, I come from a Balkan bedlam, I've fled my countrymen from whom you won't easily coax a smile, who are capable of spitting on the street like llamas in response to your *haveaniceday*, I've fled a country where the streets of life are jammed with traffic accidents . . . And look at me now! My hair is shiny and so neatly trimmed!

Meanwhile I've made the acquaintance of "my" black guy. We're sitting on a low wall in front of stores on Main Street, guzzling beer from a can.

"Don't stay," says the black guy. "You'll be black like me."

"Oh, I'm used to it," I say. "Even at home, among my own, I'm black."

"Right on," says my black. "We blacks are black everywhere."

"Black is fucking black everywhere," I say and feel myself contentedly gurgling somewhere inside: Daga-da-daga-fuck-daga-da-daga-fucking . . .

"You'll be staying here, right?" Americans often ask, never expecting a demurral.

"No," I say briefly. "Thanks. I'm unhappy, I'm fine."

Indians

We've sat down on a smooth black rock to smoke a joint. It floats from hand to hand like a silent little sailboat in the dark. There are still five minutes to go. On this grandiose stage, obscured by the darkness of Central Park, squatting on the smooth rocks, with the lake here before us, surrounded by the shimmering magic forest of skyscrapers. Paul has his arm around his lover, a gawky, boyish young man with long, frog-like legs, slightly protruding dark eyes, and pursed, moist lips, very like Pinocchio. John and Mike are perched on the rocks, slotting into each other like combs. Marushka and Melissa are standing motionless, hand in hand, their faces turned toward the skyline of Manhattan. The shades of her parents' genes, ghosts of her Czech mother and Indonesian father, tussle over Marushka's features. As though fighting a fever, Marushka buries her face in Melissa's sandy, expressionless one. Then the three of us, Mira, Goran and I. We rustle, hidden in the dark, there is no one but us and the forest of skyscrapers pressing in around Central Park. We smoke our joint and wait for the fireworks. Another three minutes to go.

Gazing at the Manhattan skyline, at the shimmering magic forest around us, we wait for the explosions. There are still two minutes to go. If I were to wind the hands of my watch forward six hours, if I were to look clear across the sky, I'd see a threatening glow on the horizon and it would be bomb shells I'd be hearing.

Istria is a peninsula with charming medieval towns, green valleys, hills, and red soil. They say the soil is rich in magnetite. The frequent mists that rise from the valleys and wreathe the medieval clock towers are caused, they say, by evaporating magnetite. There is an unusually high percentage of lunatics in Istria, far higher than in the other parts of the country. This is also ascribed to the magnetite. The Middle Ages are the only period that has left its mark on Istria: it's as if the peninsula has refused to venture into the later centuries. Today's television sets, refrigerators, satellite antennae are merely objects plucked by the magnetite vapors from the future. Compasses go haywire in Istria. I don't know about watches, but there must be a generic timepiece in Istria spinning the stuff of time in a fashion that coincides in no way with ordinary time.

The Istrian magnetite syndrome may have engulfed my whole country like a bizarre mist. It may be that fragments of history are coming back to life, attracted by the magnetite, it may be that the terrible war raging in my country is a replica of wars that already happened. Everything has been displaced, shifted, distorted like a haywire compass needle. That may be why camps spring up suddenly where former victims torture their tormentors, it may be that while traveling through time I may end up marrying my late grandfather whose head, they say, was lopped off by the sharp blow of an axe, it is not impossible that on this trip my father will be my son.

Perhaps this whole ghastly, mad, postmodern mess has been caused by the magnetite. Perhaps mysterious magnetite currents have been sucked into time and scrambled it: sabers, muskets, and bombs are swirling together, as are turbans and helmets; uniforms with an assortment of insignia are mingling, red stars are jostling with swastikas, the fascists with partisans, Rambos with medieval knights, lasers with daggers, the righteous with the wicked . . . Ages that have been revived like this are more dangerous and savage because they have lost all sense of historical continuity. The hand that raises the knife remembers the ferocity of the hatred but it no longer recalls reason or purpose. In the magnetite madness, the hand becomes more violent, strikes twice, seeks double confirmation that it's alive. Across the skies people are going readily off to their deaths as if this were a video game: they have already been through reality once and reality doesn't happen twice. People watch helplessly as heads are lopped off, the memory code is locked somewhere within them but they no longer know whether these heads are their own or their grandfathers', nor when this is truly happening. Amid the madness of haywire clocks the Balkans are navigating like an accursed ship through their own history, dreaming their warrior dreams. And for a moment I feel as if I'm sailing into a Bermuda triangle of time, into a kind of magnetite dementia, even I can no longer pinpoint where I am now: in a version of the future or my past. Because there is no longer a trustworthy reality.

This what I'm thinking about as the fireworks burst into the New York sky. On the other side of that same sky there are shells exploding and knives flashing. I feel nothing. I feel no guilt, I feel no fear. I am weightless. My companions, too, are weightless. Time is winding and spinning in directions that do not, in any case, depend on us.

We are standing in a round patch of shade, surrounded by the shadows of the bare trees. The sky above us is pink with the glow of the fireworks. We don't speak. We don't know what to do, standing in the heart of dark Central Park like fossils thrown up on a shore by the funnel of time.

And all at once, as if I've been doing it all my life, I suggest to my companions that we dance a Native American dance. "How?" they ask, eager, smiling. I reach for Pinocchio's hand, Pinocchio takes Paul's, Paul Melissa's, Melissa Mike's, Mike Marushka's . . . *Ha-ya, hayana, ha-ya-na, hayana, hayanaaa*, we chant in the darkness. I repeat steps I was taught the day before on the street by an Indian from a reservation in North Dakota. The steps are my own and so natural that I feel I've known them all my life. No one makes a mistake, no one stumbles, we dance slowly, solemnly. We dance in the night, girded by the shimmering forest of skyscrapers, crammed into the small space of the tree's shadow. It's cold, our warm breath rises in a mist from our mouths, as we, the Indians, tramp intently.

Mailbox

Amsterdam

At last I'm writing as promised, my first letter after a long spell of seclusion. I've been focusing on learning Dutch, and even more on my inner need to decide on a short- and long-term future. All this is starting to look like the vulgar version of a dream I used to have as a child—that I'd leave and never come back. But there are times when dreams invoke the future, and so it is that I've become a foreigner from nowhere, from everywhere; to the local way of thinking here I'm the ideal citizen of the world. It's beginning to look as if I'll never be able to go back, so I should try to make my peace with that as soon as possible. Expatriation from our shared cultural space does give one the benefit of distance, after all, and for that I should be thankful. At the same time this is a leap into an age-old European theme—exile—which I now need to begin to think of as my own authentic story. So far, two of my life stories have been violently interrupted: the first, my island life (seven years in Bol on the island of Brač), and the second, until recently, Belgrade. Belgrade has cracked like the last rotten egg in the Serbian basket and the stink of it has reached me even here, though I don't like to admit that. My nostrils are filled with the oppressive odor of the great, vast, and small personal apocalypse that has overwhelmed us. I used to be glad to leave Belgrade, but I was always glad to go back. Not because it was a place that was nicer for those who lived there than anywhere else, but because all journeys bring with them the desire to return to the place that owns us most and where we're able to dream about leaving forever to go to Nowhere Land—a place where there's nobody to bother us and we're completely free. But this freedom that you and I now have (because neither the national borders of our new states, nor the values within, are real yet) is not what we actually need. Hence your indecision as to your future trajectory; it will no longer be a return to a place whose immediately recognizable colors and smells refresh you and prepare you for your next escapade. It is wrenching, being utterly decentralized. We'll need to make our peace with this or—and this I do not believe will be possible for me—find a new place to return to.

As far as your brief essays are concerned, I hope you'll be able to evade the stereotypes you're so fearful of. The European in America is as blindsided as a mountaineer in the desert. It takes time before first the gaze and then the imagination begin to live with the new influx of values.

Since this letter is slipping ever more rapidly down the diverse meanders of my agitated mind and I'd prefer to be able to talk this over with you in person, and although this has no real beginning or end, I'll stop here with warm greetings, Yours, P.

Zagreb

. . . Goran is the only one who's doing well. The war hasn't affected him much, he even finds going down into the shelter fun, there are a lot of children there he can play war games with. He's well-equipped for war because I bought him a helmet of the so-called "Yugoslav People's Army," and a beret like the ones our sailors currently wear, and all that makes him top dog in the building. H. is writing his book and playing Tetris a lot. That's how he shields himself from the television, which is always on. The problem, as ever, is money. The new currency reminds me of Monopoly money. The notes are so small and nondescript that you spend them without a qualm. Yours, S.

. . . It's Saturday morning, S. is in the big room, sitting at the small table in front of the television, a cigarette and decaf coffee beside her. She's writing you a letter. I asked her to leave space for me to write to you as well. She said: there's not going to be any space, write your own letter. So I'm at the computer (in the bedroom now) writing you my own letter. Goran is in his room, lying on the floor, surrounded by felt-tip pens, and he is writing you his own letter. I have harnessed all the writerly individualism in this little family workshop for which you are the target audience. Yours, H.

. . . So, I smoke like a chimney, I'm dog-tired and constantly hungry. I could eat a horse. Altogether I've become a strange beast. What can I say—our new state is like a fairy tale. A good fairy came, waved its magic wand and turned us into . . . Europeans. In order to be seen as such, we now have singers on television dressed as princesses and princes. The ceremonial guard is looking like tin soldiers. The refugees from Vukovar were taken to Hotel Intercontinental to be filmed for television, and now they're in sports halls, sleeping on mats. Yours, S.

. . . This thing with S. is genuinely amazing: he writes without pressure, without preparatory rituals (pacing, fraying nerves, frequent declarations that it's high time to start), he writes in chapters and announces this with glee. When the air-raid warnings stopped, everyday life became easier. That is, life became commonplace in a familiar way: the astronomical prices, the rock-bottom salaries (mine is 200 DM), the cost of living soaring every day . . . Yours, H.

. . . As far as work is concerned, the situation is appalling. I've made a TV play and four documentaries. None of them have been screened. I'm working on two plays, but I'm not sure they'll be produced. Meanwhile tax policy is such that if you earn, say, a hundred thousand, you'll get fifty, so it's hardly worth working. The best thing seems to be smuggling, and a lot of people are doing it . . . Yours, S.

. . . But now there's a new element in people's mood and behavior. Instead of the despair of inflation, people are reaching, inventing ways of scraping together some kind of income. Your reflexes are different when you're trying to drag yourself bit by bit out of a fundamental evil and when you're falling gradually into shit. In fact people are complaining a lot less than they used to. They've become calculating, resourceful, and when things go wrong they say, "Fuck that."
An indication of their increased resourcefulness is the large number of thefts, break-ins, and looting. It's not just that war inevitably leads to an erosion of moral standards, this is also about the survival instinct. Our neighbor F. told me about a recent bank raid. A masked man went into a bank with a machine gun and shouted: "Everyone down on the floor!" The people looked at him in astonishment. He fired into the air and shouted: "Down on the floor!" Down they dropped. Then he realized there was no one left to hand him over the money. He kicked a poor man on the floor and ordered him to hand over the

money. The man asked: "Is it okay if I crawl?" This upset the bank robber and he rushed out of the bank. Yours, H.

. . . I was at the market. Broccoli costs 4 marks, a head of lettuce almost 8 marks, no one buys bananas any more, not to mention meat, there's plenty of meat. Salaries are at about 200 marks and that's considered a decent wage. Anything you earn over two hundred is taxed additionally. There are no more imports in the stores, so you wouldn't be able to buy your cigarettes, just so you know, and I can't find any decaf coffee. If you're lucky you can still buy these things on the coast, there are still imports there. In Dubrovnik they have Marlboros but no electricity and water . . . Yours, S.

. . . I have to stop now, the letter mustn't be too thick and I don't know how to print on both sides of the page on this printer (lent us by F., our neighbor). Bye. Yours, H.

. . . Goran is very attached to me. I can't go anywhere without him asking where I'm going and when I'll be back. I've just sent him away because he was sitting, staring at my letter, which was a total distraction. He just got over the flu, which everyone in Zagreb but me has had. Now I've got to go and make dinner, it's my turn today. Do you ever hear from J. in Belgrade? How is she? And the children? If she gets in touch do send her our best wishes. Warmest greetings from us all, especially the child, who's writing to you himself. Yours, S.

. . . Dear Duba, I really liked the cat you sent. Next time you write please tell me when you're coming back from America. I've just had the flu and I'm still coughing and have a runny nose but I'm back at school. School's okay, it's boring at home. Lots of love,

Goran

Belgrade

. . . You seem so far away, and I miss you more than when you used to leave on your earlier jaunts. The trouble is probably that life went on in an ordinary way back then, while so much has changed now in our lives. Sometimes I feel this could settle down, that our lives could once again have at least a steadier footing, other times the whole of our past seems so distant, yet there are times when I feel it might all somehow renew itself. I don't know. As you see, the conditional has become part of my style. This is our garb these days, we add it like a stylish touch to what others have designed and tailored for us.

When I take stock of everything, I don't have the impression that living in this part of the world is going to be comfortable. I'm afraid of the bitterness that has built up in everyone, I'm afraid of the search for proof of loyalty to "the great ideas" for which we've fought, I'm afraid, in the final analysis, of the material poverty which will mark the life of these lands for years to come. God, how it all sickens me.

Forgive me for beginning this letter on such a dark note, but the war in Bosnia has been raging for several days now. And it doesn't help that sane people there, in far greater numbers than anywhere else in this wretched country, have gone out into the streets demanding not to be herded into ethnic corrals by nationality, but to be left alone to live in peace; they went to the barricades barehanded, thinking this the ultimate and irrefutable argument, but this is a logic that resides elsewhere. Here people shoot into unarmed crowds; those who sought peace were chased back to their homes, and now Bosnia is burning. I don't know what to tell you, except that I'm truly desperate. I'd hoped it wouldn't come to this. I'd hoped the blue helmets would be peacefully deployed and we'd manage to reestablish at least some semblance of normal life: that V. would be able to come here, and I'd be free go to Zagreb . . .

I'm overcome by a crushing grief and nostalgia for Zagreb, particularly now that everything is heating up again and it seems so far away. I remember all those nice things that made our lives what they were and I wonder whether any of that will persist once peace does return, or at least something we'll call peace. At the moment what I miss most is contact with those I love. I can't reach anyone by phone, because you can't get through until after midnight, and then with difficulty, so I only call V. There wasn't any mail delivered for a long time, and even now it's not reliable. I do receive greetings from people now and then, but it's so little. And time goes by so quickly, I simply can't believe so much time has passed since I left.

The situation grows worse by the day in Bosnia, the future is more and more uncertain. For days now I haven't been able to reach V. by phone and I just hope this is only temporary. It meant a lot to be able to hear his voice, to know how he was . . . I don't know how S. and H. are either. If you're in touch with them, send them my love. I'll stop now and continue some other time.

Yours, J.

Couch Potato

At the end of January last year I spent a few days in Gothenburg. Every day I'd go down to the dining room for breakfast, pick up a coffee and a roll, and settle down in the hotel lobby. There I'd watch the American war reports from Iraq. On the screen the war looked like a video game, all the more so because the same news reports kept recycling. Indifferent to the war in the Gulf, I sipped my coffee and munched my breakfast. For me the Gulf War was the size of a cup of coffee and a Swedish roll.

At the end of May last year I found myself in a crowd of people on the main Zagreb square. On the open stage there was a succession of speakers with operetta-like faces, musicians, singers, girls in folk costumes. It was hot and sticky, the voices jangled harshly in the loudspeakers, the town pigeons flapped their wings nervously. I felt suddenly uneasy and went home, pulled down the blinds, and switched on the television. You could see everything better on the screen, but it looked different somehow. The newly elected president was performing a bizarre pantomime: he placed a coin in an empty baby's cradle. People laid their hands on their chests in the vicinity of their hearts and sobbed with emotion. At first I thought the pictures were coming from another country, another city, and then, perhaps, from another age. Only, had this age already been or was it yet to come?

I spent last July in my Zagreb apartment, the shutters closed, transfixed by the television screen. The numbing effect of the images dulled the dread tightening like an invisible noose in the air. A series of movies from India was running on television. I'd turn off the sound and curl up on my couch, watch Indian women making Os with their mouths, knitting their brows in Vs, tossing back their black braids, lashing the male characters with passionate looks, breathing rapidly and casting sideways glances, like rabbits. Utterly stricken by the heat and dread, I watched Indian men scowl, cross their arms, sigh, arch their eyebrows in Ws, and lash the female characters with glances full of dark longing.

While the invisible noose tightened over the city, I lay curled up on the couch, picking up Indian gestures, perusing the register of Indian emotions as if studying a textbook. I stared at the screen as though at any moment it would emit a distant signal, a message of salvation. I spent last August in a little island village on the Adriatic. There was just one small bakery in the village and in it there was a small television set, as big as a largish matchbox. In the evening all the locals congregated there. The children clamored noisily for ice cream; the proprietor, an Albanian, juggled the ice cream scoops without taking his eyes from the screen, while we grown-ups stood shoulder to shoulder, hypnotized by the black-and-white image. Each evening the little screen splashed us with a wave of black-and-white evil. The scenes of war looked more terrible on the little television set, black-and-white was more terrible than color, more terrible at night than by day.

I spent last September in my Zagreb apartment. A bag with the essentials stood by the front door. At the sound of the air-raid siren I'd grab it and run down to the cellar. In the cellar I felt like an extra in a war movie. In the evening, in my darkened apartment, I switched on the television and watched houses in ruins, tear-stained faces, corpses and carcasses. I often heard gunfire. I would turn down the volume so I could check to hear whether the gunshots were coming from outside on the street or from my television screen.

I spent last November in New York in an apartment belonging to a friend who was away. I hardly went out, I watched television. The image on the screen was often accompanied by the sound of police sirens reaching me from the street.

In December I temporarily rented a small room from Gail in Middletown. On one wall of the room hung a framed letter from Samuel Beckett thanking her for choosing him as the subject of her doctoral thesis. Gail was hardly ever home so I spent most of my time in the kitchen rather than in my room. From the little television set, the size of a largish matchbox, installed above the kitchen sink, came a steady stream of incomprehensible little black-and-white images. For some reason I had the nagging feeling that I was actually in Moscow. Whether it was because of the yellowing oil paint on the kitchen walls or because of time passing more slowly, I don't know.

Four years ago, during my last visit to Moscow, I didn't call my Moscow friends as usual. Most of the time I spent in my hotel room, hidden behind thick, plush curtains, watching television.

On the screen were a succession of shots of Gorbachev, interminable programs about the hypnotist Koshpirovsky who'd hypnotized millions of Soviet citizens over television, and lazy shots in programs on how to arrange food tastefully. I stared at the sad sprigs of parsley on the screen and for some reason felt I was about to die.

I would watch to the end of the day's programming and the weather forecast. The gentle voice of the announcer and soft music accompanied frozen photographs of Soviet cities in which the mercury had fallen to thirty degrees below zero. Lying in my darkened room in the dim light coming from the screen I thought of Nadezhda Mandelstam, who wrote somewhere that during the Stalinist purges—numb with fear in the face of the invisible Russian roulette whistling over their heads—people spent most of their time lying down.

At the end of December last year I moved into my temporary Middletown apartment and immediately ordered cable TV. I moved the couch so I could watch television while lying down. Since then for days I've been watching American women making Os with their mouths, and American men knitting their brows in Vs. I've been picking up American gestures, perusing the register of American emotions as though studying a textbook. American television is like a vast classroom for visual instruction.

Some American analyses show that a large percentage of American children fail to distinguish daily life from television reality. This does not seem to be the children's fault. I myself have trouble with this. Reality is imitating the screen and the screen reality, with ever more success. Besides, reality or screen, it doesn't matter, what matters is to *stay tuned.*

I'm bothered by something else. It's the lack of synchrony that irks me, there seems to be a rupture between emotional response and what provoked the response, inappropriate emotions. For some time now I've become increasingly attuned to such ruptures. In a movie a while ago I saw actors bent over a fresh corpse. Instead of knitting their brows in an anxious V, they stretched their faces into a grin. Yet at the same time they were saying: "Terrible, terrible." As if they'd arrived late, as if they'd forgotten to put on the appropriate emotional mask, as if the director hadn't given them clear instructions.

I saw a program recently in which ordinary people, contestants, wept over shopping carts crammed with fat turkeys and gigantic boxes of detergent, they wept as though they had been struck by a shocking natural disaster. Their faces expressed profound emotion, their bodies wracked with sincere sobs. The cause of this powerful emotional response was their win in a shopping contest which brought them a few hundred dollars and a shopping cart heaped with trophy goodies.

Directors anticipate the possible absence of the expected response in a comedy show with "canned laughter." Ads control any possible absence of aesthetic response with stern and unambiguous slogans: *This is beautiful!* But what about other emotional responses? Especially since life imitates the screen, and the screen—life?

"How are you doing?" asks my American friend Norman.
"Awful," I say.
"Great," he says and thumps me heartily on the shoulder. "Oh, I'm sorry," he adds belatedly, arching his brows in a V.

Sometimes I feel as if I have a film editor's desk in my head. I organize the images, correct the spoiled emotional mechanisms. I edit out the shots of the weeping American supermarket contestants and add in pictures from the massacres at home. And so on. I introduce a natural order. And then, weary, I give up. Who am I, I think, to judge human emotions and edit mechanisms? Besides, I myself have changed, I no longer like getting calls from home when they tell me terrible things, when they tell me that 500 shells fell on Osijek that day. How awful, I say, it snowed here. And I realize that I have uttered the sentence quite naturally, without a thought, that my tele-brain has begun to give everything in the world the same weight or lightness, everyone has the right to an equal number of seconds, each of us has our sound bite, in one shot someone is devouring a hamburger, in another, someone is dying. All that matters is to *stay tuned.*

Bela was 29 and Janos Lazar 31 when they closed their door and began watching television. They didn't leave their house for a full 39 years, said the newspaper article about the couch-potato couple from Savannah. "We are quite content just watching our TV," said the Lazars.

I'm lying on my couch, the calendar says it's the end of February. My face has grown gray, I'm drying up inside, I am a couch potato. I think of the way the world is going to the devil, sliding serenely into a white hell of indifference. I think of the fact that the world is nothing but a screen and we are either actors or audience, no matter which; someone is confidently directing us, and, besides, who cares. The world is a *soap-noir*, and this is its ultimate genre, the image that Earth, as it collapses like a dead star, will long send off into space.

I lie here like this, I no longer turn off the television. Sometimes I wake up at night and smile: the empty screen is looking at me from the corner of the room. Snow drifts from the screen into the room. It falls slowly, covering me like a blanket. With the last vestige of consciousness I register the gentle voice of the announcer. In Irkutsk it is thirty degrees below zero, in Florida—eighty above. Languages gurgle and merge, smiling and tear-stained faces overlay each other, the living and the dead, towns that come into being and towns that disappear, geographical points merge, the Amazon flows into the Black Sea, the Volga into the Atlantic. Earth revolves slowly like an empty screen from which snow drifts. *Stay tuned.*

Yugo-Americana

At a party I happened to attend recently, I shook hands with Lauren Bacall. For Lauren Bacall I was just another silent, anonymous hand. For me her handshake meant far more—among other things it was the symbolic closing of a cultural circle.

Lauren Bacall could not have known that I was coming from Yugoslavia and that the culture of my childhood consisted of Greek myths, Partisan tales, and Hollywood movies. In the fifties, Hollywood movies compensated abundantly for the shortage of children's books. Yugoslavia was a country impoverished by war and, apparently, printing children's books cost more than importing Hollywood films, which flooded the country like a propaganda bonus. As a result, instead of Peter Pan and Winnie the Pooh, other stars shone in the sky of my childhood. Among them, Lauren Bacall.

When people do not know the culture of other countries, which is almost always the case, they replace knowledge with cultural stereotype. A stereotype is a little mythic structure, a sort of directional signal on the broadly branching map of the languages, religions, ideologies, and cultures. Contemporary cultures produce myths about themselves: the strongest media machines produce the most powerful myths. Then once the myth is entrenched, teasing out whether reality produced the cultural myth—or the myth reality—becomes a challenge. Once entrenched, the cultural myth becomes an object of both contention and affirmation, both rejection and reinforcement. In short, the myth becomes a fundamental premise of the cultural system. Like a genre, it generates itself and furthers its existence in new cultural products: movies, television, books, fashion, music, art. Cultural myths seem to come into being at the fertile nexus of the links between art, popular culture, everyday life, politics, ideology, the habitus. And it is precisely these deep links that make them myths and not merely a cultural corpus connected by kindred subject-matter.

One of the greatest myths of the twentieth century is that of Americana, the image America has of itself, which came into being in the mid-twentieth century somewhere between Hollywood and Madison Avenue. The myth created over the years reached its crowning sophistication in Warhol's painting of the Campbell's Soup can and has been repeated ever since in movies, novels, television, and, once again, in life. Today it is not entirely clear whether millions of people are slurping soup or . . . myth.

The American cultural myth knocked at the door of postwar Yugoslavia in 1953. That was the year Yugoslav cinemas showed the American movie *Water Ballet* with Esther Williams in the leading role. Esther, of course, had no idea that her shapely swimmer's legs had symbolically kicked shut the door on an uninvited guest—Soviet Socialist Realism. In 1948, Tito had spoken his famous NO to Stalin, and Esther Williams, a pioneer of the ideological struggle against hard-core communism, served as the most effective propaganda confirmation that Tito was right.

America arrived in postwar Yugoslavia not only with UNRRA packages, Truman's eggs, milk, and cheddar cheese (I still buy cheddar today out of nostalgia, recalling the orange triangles we were given at school as a snack), but also with Hollywood movies and translated books: Sinclair Lewis, Upton Sinclair, Theodore Dreiser, John Dos Passos, Irving Stone, Hemingway. In the sixties it bubbled up with the Kerouacs, Salingers, Ginsburgs . . . And when television sets entered every home, the screen may have shrunk but America grew. It showered every household like longed-for rain: with television series and soap operas, with the Peyton Places, the McClouds, Dallases, Dynasties, and Santa Barbaras.

American culture came as it came: reduced, fragmented, fed by images from the small and big screens; it came with the media, newspapers, cartoons, music, books, popular culture, symbols, but also with a flesh-and-blood media army—returning émigrés, ship captains, sailors, migrant workers, the children of émigrés. And so it permeated local daily life. In the fifties, in a small provincial cinema, sitting on a wooden bench that had no backrest, my mother held my hand and greedily drank in the images from the screen. At first I didn't understand a thing. Later, as a child of eight, I was smitten with Audie Murphy, the hero of American westerns. This diminutive man who'd been decorated with 22 war medals for valor, with his round childish face, was the postwar Yugoslav Superman. At ten I callously dumped Audie, replacing him with Marlon Brando, Brando with James Dean, Dean with Anthony Perkins . . . I also remember the sweet children's trading cards of Hollywood stars we used to find in chewing-gum packages. Whoever filled their album with a complete set was master of unimaginable wealth. Letters were written to Tony

Curtis and answers received. Signed photographs were displayed in places of honor. This was the time of the first Yugo-pop songs that were, in fact, American. The lyrics abounded with exciting words such as *prairie*, *cactus*, *my little horse*, *revolver*, *my sweetheart* . . . In the fifties we soaked up everything from the movie screen: words, fashion, music, interior design. In that age before ready-made clothes, people had their clothes sewn to order and women would frequently ask their seamstresses to make them a suit like the one Doris Day wore in the movie *Pillow Talk*. And the seamstresses knew exactly what kind of suit they meant.

With the appearance of *Peyton Place*, the Yugoslav television viewer acquired years of entertainment. As a little girl I identified with the character of the teenage girl, Alison, played by Mia Farrow. I walked along the streets of my little provincial town with a notebook forever tucked under my arm, just as Mia Farrow did through her Peyton.

At local flea-markets you could buy cheap, secondhand, American goods diligently sent by American émigrés to their poor relations. I gazed enviously at the clothes my friend Lidija had been sent by her émigré grandmother. So I'd feel better, my mother bought me a little organdy dress from America at the flea market. Who knows why, it looked a lot like an Austrian dirndl. When my friend received a large package containing a worn red windbreaker with a hood and her first jeans, my heart totally broke from envy. With the jeans and her red windbreaker, my friend could have had any boy she wanted.

Perhaps the history of the American myth in postwar Yugoslav culture can best be illustrated by small details: the first postwar translations of American books were full of footnotes. Everything had to be explained: what a jukebox was, what marijuana was, and what jeans were. The footnotes (of the type: *jukebox*, a machine that plays music when a small coin is inserted) began to disappear, gradually at first, then ever more rapidly, because these unknown things were becoming more and more a part of everyday reality. The world had apparently become a global village. Perhaps it had become a global **American** village, I won't go into that. All in all, the same movies were featured at the same time in theaters in New York and Zagreb, my mother and my American friend Norman's mother, Edith, watched *The Golden Girls* on television at the same time in their respective homes.

Besides, in a way people began to resemble one another. In the movie *Working Girl* I was touched by Melanie Griffith's friend with her pink-and-pale-blue synthetic wedding, so like our own. I was overcome by a feeling of deep understanding in the scene in which the two of them, looking through their rich boss's wardrobe, find an elegant black dress. "That must have cost six hundred dollars!" says Melanie in awe. "And it's not even leather!" says her friend, disappointed.

Perhaps for the same reason I was touched by the malicious Alexis rebuking her lover in a scene from *Dynasty*. In her grand bathtub, they're sipping champagne and eating caviar. At one moment Alexis exclaims: "That's caviar, not peanut butter!" The remark was not, in fact, intended for her lover but for the millions of Americans who had to be reminded of yet another stereotype of wealth. I was touched by the thought of those for whom the television screen really was a window onto a more beautiful, finer, more brilliant world. Norman's mother in Detroit and my mother in Zagreb were in that sense equally dwelling in the global village.

Perhaps it was this same sense of a loose global W that spurred my colleague Pavao Pavličić to write a short story entitled "Return to Hannibal." The story was published in the 1980s and describes parallel worlds, the little town of Hannibal on the Mississippi and little town of Vukovar on the Danube. Hannibal and Vukovar are like communicating vessels, the houses are the same, the people are the same, the lives and events unfold in them in parallel. Everything that happens in Vukovar on the Danube occurs at the same time in Hannibal on the Mississippi. Today, just under four years later, this story which until recently did not have the dimension of fantasy is no longer plausible. For if the logic of the real world were to follow the logic of Pavličić's story, the town of Hannibal on the Mississippi would have been razed to the ground by now. In just one year reality has brutally destroyed the idea of the sameness of various worlds. A bloody reality produced the Balkan Myth once long ago, and today this Balkan Myth is producing our bloody reality.

Unpredictable reality continues its game with myths. From here I observe the media reinforcing the Balkan Myth as it is gradually constructed from newspaper photographs and TV news reports. The television shots of desperate, wretched, disheveled people, their eyes wild, dovetail perfectly with the Balkan stereotype. And no one seems to ask why so many of these desperate people have a decent command of the English language. At the same time as the myth of the wild Balkans is being constructed here (after all, reality is not offering up alternatives), people in the Balkans themselves continue to live the American myth! Balkan reality refuses to conform to its own image, it prefers the American one! And so, in slang, a knife is called a rambo, Croatian soldiers wear bands around their foreheads to look like Sylvester Stallone, the town of Knin is known as Knin Peaks, and the Serbian paramilitaries are Kninjas. Reality is swiftly being immortalized not only in new songs composed in the style of the oral epic tradition, but also in the deeply American genre of comic strips. Murderers like Serbian Captain Dragan are the heroes of comics today; they wield a knife while on their feet they're wearing Reeboks! In Belgrade slang, Belgrade is now known as Arkansas. Arkan is the name of a murderer, a confectioner by trade, a famous hunter of Croatian heads.

And besides, while I watch horrific American television images of the destruction of Sarajevo, my mother in Zagreb is watching *Santa Barbara*. And while the tanned actors utter their lines, their expressions numbed by boredom, promiscuity, and movement through confined spaces, breaking-news banners often flash across on the screen: air-raid danger in Zadar, air-raid danger in Karlovac, air-raid danger in Slavonski Brod . . .
So the Balkan reality identifies not with the Balkan Myth but, once again, with the American one. The difference is only in the deaths, the genuine, homegrown, *Balkan* variety. At the same time many Americans still believe that the deaths "down there" in the Balkans are celluloid deaths. Not all of them do, of course. Certainly not Lauren Bacall.

Body

Golden-yellow orange juice glistens in a sunlit glass; a thick, sweet layer of caramel slides down hillocks of pinkish ice cream; with a ripping sound the zip on a pair of jeans makes its way up toward a belly button bedewed with golden droplets of sweat; a succulent behind displays its pear-shaped form; thick, red sauce oozes, drenching thirsty pasta; pearly teeth sink into an apple with a juicy crunch; waterfalls of silken curls cascade down a woman's gentle shoulders; oatmeal flakes drop with a silent crash into a milky sea with porcelain shores; and it's all so *juicy,* ah, all so *crispy,* mmm, all so *crunchy,* mmmm, all so *fluffy,* mmmm, all so *delicious,* ohhh, all so *irresistible.*

I adore American commercials. American ads are the condensed, perfectly designed ideology of American daily life. They zero in on and nurture the fundamental substance of American life. And the fundamental substance of American life (and every other life, only no one else has realized it!) is the body. The BODY! The eating, walking, sleeping, moving body. This straightforward message—the b-o-d-y—pours out of television screens sprinkled through a multi-colored carnival of images.

American ads zero in on and service every part of the body in turn. Most often and above all they appeal to the *mouth*. They recommend which cereal Americans should shovel into their mouths, which cookies they should munch, which processed food they should consume, which drinks they should sip, which candy they should nibble. They teach Americans what to put into their bodies.

If one group of ads concerns itself wholeheartedly with *filling*, another is zealously occupied with *emptying*. Advertisements dealing with uncomfortable abdominal pain alternate with ads for hamburgers, advertisements for bloating with ads for candy, advertisements for laxatives with ads for juice, advertisements for hemorrhoids with those for cheeses.

While one group of ads treats the body like a machine for digesting, another is concerned with how to bring this sated body into optimal shape: how to slim it down, how to divest it of superfluous fat, how to mold it, how to make it dynamic *(Move your body!* commands one slogan), how to train it, how to bring it to perfection.

American celebrity Jane Fonda advertises her very own invention—a small, cheap, plastic step for shaping the leg muscles—displaying the very same touching solemnity with which she once protested against the war in Vietnam.

If a photograph in the *New York Times* of a beautiful body with the caption "Body Consciousness" (whatever that means) is given several times larger than a photograph of fresh corpses somewhere in Bosnia, then it is quite n-o-r-m-a-l that an American (and this happened to me) would go on exercising while you answer his question about "that war in the Balkans." Or that the person with whom you're conversing (this happened to me, too) leaps up from her chair in a restaurant and spontaneously performs a few exercises to stretch her back while you're talking about postmodernism for which she, the person with whom you're talking, otherwise professes a passionate interest.

Work on the body is not yet done. American commercials also offer Americans abundant advice about how they should cherish their sated and beautifully toned body—*Nourish it inside, nourish it outside* recommends one ambiguously rhythmic TV slogan. Ads talk about skin, hair, teeth, legs, face. American TV screens gush with bath foams, shampoos, perfumes, lotions.

Hearing that I was from "Eastern Europe," one American woman immediately asked me in earnest, "Do you have The Body Shop over there?"

My student Alyosha from Irkutsk told me a story. Before students from the (former) Soviet Union went off to study at American universities, the American organizers of the exchange program arranged a brief orientation for them. The American side gave each student a bar of soap, a towel, deodorant, and a sheet of paper with instructions about behavior in America. The first paragraph said that Americans were a "clean" people, that they took showers every day (even more than one!) so the Soviet students were asked to follow this pattern themselves, to use deodorant and change their underwear daily.

There is, therefore (*clean*) America and then—the *others*. At the frontier between these two worlds I imagine Woody Allen as the customs officer. Why him? Because somewhere he described a nightmare in which bad people broke into his apartment to shampoo him!

Work on the body is not yet done. Now your immediate surroundings must be put in order. There are many ads recommending how consumers should clean the space around them: what to use for cleaning the kitchen, the bathroom, dust, windows, dishes, laundry, what to use for the toilet bowl. These stir in female viewers a deeply rooted, child's dream of a dollhouse, so it's no wonder that one New York landlady who was renting an apartment to a compatriot of mine showed him a pillowcase and sheet and said in an instructive tone: "This is a pillowcase, we, Americans, insert the pillow in it, and this is a sheet, we, Americans, spread it on the bed."

And when everything is, at last, clean both inside and out, American ads advise Americans to place their sated, toned, nurtured body—in a car. The only advertisement concerned with the non-corporeal sphere of American life is one teaching Americans how to telephone efficiently and save. The other human activities, judging by the ads, of course, are quite unimportant. There are just a few advertising messages concerning travel (recreation of the body!), the selection of credit cards (to pay for all the body has consumed), and so on.

In American culture, the body is treated like His Excellency the Body. The American ideology of the body will therefore do all it can to remove and destroy the old-fashioned, shameful *multiple meanings* that the idea of the body implies. So it is that the images on the screen of bald men who shortly thereafter boast a full head of hair are devoid of even the slightest hint of parody: the ads for hairpieces and transplants are advertisements like any others. Ads with buxom beauties are aired alongside shots of heaps of thousands of discarded silicone breasts, but it will not occur to anyone to make the ironic link between the two. Alongside ads for gleaming teeth there are ads for artificial denture gum: the perfect design of both destroys any notion of an ironic contrast.

With its ideology of the body, America strips the body of its right to carnival-grotesque ambivalence. Images traverse the TV screen of a contest to find the fattest American woman or the ugliest face in America, but television, that potent shaper of collective thinking, destroys every ironic-subversive message. The contest for the fattest American woman is not to be interpreted as the carnival revolt of the ugly body pitted against the beautiful, or at least serving as its logical opposite; instead it functions as a democratic permit issued by democratic America allowing the existence of alternatives, variants. And the contest participants themselves present not as ugly, but as *alternatively* beautiful women.

Notions—no matter how bizarre—that have sprung from this same ideology are devoid of irony as well, such as ideas about hibernation or mummification of the body, and so forth. For instance, the lawyers on *L.A. Law* treat with the utmost gravity a case of a client who wishes to be mummified after his death!

In its ideology of the unambiguous body, America has deftly eliminated all opposites: illness, ageing, death, ugliness, physical decay. America builds its ideology of the body on infantile mechanisms (besides, does only the body require sophistication?). This collective American body is like a baby that feeds, burps, shits, pees, takes its first steps, and receives the enthusiastic acclaim of its surroundings. Almost all ads satisfy the infantile level of existence: the most explicit is one promoting measures to counteract diarrhea (or constipation, it doesn't matter). The husband is leaving for work with an anxious expression; his wife, with a look that "knows all and understands," hands him pills. In the next shot the husband phones home from work: all trace of offended annoyance has been erased: he is smiling, relaxed, confident. Bravo, applauds his wife's face. Bravo, applaud the millions of American TV viewers.

Every bodily victory in the American pioneering myth, five hundred years old and still youthful, receives the approval of its surroundings. Michael Jackson—symbol of the American body that designs and redesigns itself, metamorphoses, turns from black to white, a body reaching for eternity—receives widespread applause. Bravo, Michael, bravo, victorious body.

Willa Scott—a centenarian who attends a daily belly-dancing class, coquettishly undulating her old-lady belly—earns the applause of America. *What's the secret of living so long?* Americans ask Willa Scott. And it doesn't occur to anyone to ask: *What's the purpose of living so long?* Longevity is an end in itself. Bravo, Willa! Bravo, long-living body!

Women and men who go in for bodybuilding, known, without irony, as beefcakes, earn the applause of their surroundings. Bravo, body! In the most crowded New York streets, you can see a lone young man stop, put down his bag, take out his weights and start pumping. At night in New York you can see individuals in sports clothes stopping beside walls, stairs, concrete blocks, and stretching while taking no notice of anything or anyone. These isolated exercisers work their muscles in the New York night. As if they need no one, as if they're sufficient unto themselves. Perhaps unconsciously they're emitting signals, perhaps the quiver of their muscles, traversing light years, will provoke a tender vibration on some other planet. These isolated exercisers, samurai warriors, these who have abandoned the sanctioned places—fitness centers, parks, beaches, open and closed exercise areas—and have spread throughout American space are simply radicalizing the idea of the beautiful, healthy, dynamic, and autistic body. For the American body communicates with no one and serves no purpose.

This is to say that the American ideology of body has deprived the alluring body of its right to association, its sexual function, it has deprived the sexually attractive body of its right to sexual attraction. This deprivation of function has been institutionalized by the law on harassment: every thought, even the most innocent, of the sexual use of the body has become punishable. And the mental castration of the sexual function has freed space for new functions.

A new advertisement for Reebok sneakers promotes a strong and independent female body, ready for the most demanding physical exploits. *Life is short, play it hard*, advises the slogan. The ad seems to suggest a new function—the warrior—for the body. As though a future America will be ruled by strong women-warriors wearing Reeboks instead of armor.

The mental castration of the sexual function of the body opens up room for new aesthetic functions. The asexual body becomes a sculpture. The rejected fetish of the breast (bequeathed by either bountiful nature or the silicone industry) has been replaced today by the fetish of the arm, and for this we are, ourselves, responsible. Like every *objet d'art*, the sculpted arm soon found its promoters, its philosophers, critics, its artistic workshops. "Self-determination," says Radu, the artistic director of a studio for physical culture in Manhattan. "Discipline and power," recommends Pat Manocchia, Madonna's personal trainer. Pump-up aesthetics, self-determination, these are the new terms, and bodily beauty is being redefined. "Beauty today is the muscle in motion—living, active, graceful tissue, like a cobra," says Radu the aesthete.

In the disrupted, sexually castrated system of values, it can happen that a glance at a turkey, as plump as a harem beauty, lying outspread (always on its back!) in the freezers of American supermarkets, may stir a blush, and the sight of a built-up muscle makes the mouth water! Is something wrong? And is this perhaps the reason why the harem turkey is wrapped, to no effect, in polythene packaging that, in fact, simply emphasizes its curves? Is something wrong? Everything's fine. One of the logical notions produced by the American system of disrupted functions of the body is cannibalism. If the body is not to serve certain functions, why shouldn't it serve others?

Besides, who would dream of eating a starving African child, a sallow Chinaman, a desiccated Turk who smokes a hundred cigarettes a day, or a wretch who has been massacring people in the Balkans? But the American body, beautiful, healthy, and so pointless . . . with those biceps and triceps, lively, active, and as graceful as a cobra . . . Mmm, that's so *juicy*, mmmm, so *fluffy*, so *crispy*, mmm, *irresistible* . . .

After all, the substitution of the whole by the part, the body by the fetish of the arm, satisfies the gourmet principles of cannibalism. No cannibal up to now has ever eaten the whole body, not even Chikatilo. Andrei Chikatilo, the Russian cannibal who ate 56 people, was given vast publicity in American media. "I am a mistake of nature, a mad beast," proclaimed the cannibal from Rostov in the American version. Chikatilo went on to announce that his cannibalism was the result of "sexual inadequacy and the repressive Soviet system." Chikatilo (with George Bush) not only delivered the final blow to communism, but introduced a new, political aspect to the sophisticated American cannibalism of silent lambs and American psychos.

His Excellency the Body . . . I come from a country in which the body is no more than a cheap target. When I got here, of course, I immediately rushed off to an aerobics class, ordered a Nordic Track, filled my kitchen cupboards with SlimFast, and I have a Thigh Master rolling pornographically around in a corner. And then I realized it was too late and gave up. I'm too old, indoctrinated, inured to the idea that the body is worthless, no more than a cheap target. The everyday reality in my terrible country is constantly confirming this. Human bodies are used in my country to fertilize the soil, to feed the chickens and pigs, bodies fill pits so that one day, from them will spring again the fat black seed of evil.

Actually, I didn't give up entirely.

A little while ago, I read an ad in my local newspaper. Roger Papazian from nearby Rocky Hill was advertising an unusual service at Eden, his business. And so, when I die, please have me cremated, and then place my ashes not in an urn, but in the hands of Mr. Papazian. He promises he will use my ashes to fill bullets. I, an incorrigibly idle slob, will at last have a satisfactory body: slender, seductive, aerodynamic and dangerous. At last I'll be "slim as an arrow"! And where I end up—in the heart of an aged lover, in the body of an enemy, or some innocent wild duck—is quite unimportant. Because the body is eternal. Only the spirit is perishable.

Harassment

As a foreigner in America I found many challenges to figure out. I figured out how to use coupons for supermarket shopping; I managed to shop by television, telephone, and catalogue; I came to understand what those famous 1-800 numbers were for and how to react when the manic voice of an answering machine instructs you how to call another answering machine; I learned how to make collect calls, and even how to change phone companies and why. I puzzled out a few things about taxation, a terrible headache for Americans as well as foreigners. I no longer push my fingers into the drain in the kitchen sink when the garbage disposal is on, yes, I worked that one out, too. And as soon as I moved in I switched off the smoke detectors. I smoke and I know how sensitive they are to smokers. That, too, I learned.

I can identify with many major American problems. Hate crimes, for instance—I know all about those. I have a feel for the problems of American intellectualism and anti-intellectualism, the feminization of American culture and its renewed masculinization. What is mainstream, the class system in America, the electoral system, the culture of American daily life, none of these are entirely unfamiliar to me. I understand everything that begins with multi- (multicultural, multinationalism, and multimillionaires); all the -isms, from adhoc-ism to consumerism; I'm conversant with everything post-, from post-communism to post-colonialism. I have some notion of new age, self-esteem, virtual reality, the New World Order, globalization, and the like. I'm even beginning to get the hang of American baseball, incomprehensible to many foreigners.

There's only one thing I cannot grasp: harassment. The fact that my English-Croatian dictionary explains harassment as meaning "torment, annoyance, bother, disturbance, repeated attack" doesn't tell me much. I'm grateful to an American colleague who kindly gave me guidelines, a pamphlet with illustrations so that even the illiterate can follow, but still I don't! Studying the pamphlet I found, for instance, that harassment is divided into verbal, non-verbal, and physical abuse. Verbal harassment has to do with threats and insults, offensive or suggestive comments, messages of a sexual nature, insisting on intimate meetings, offensive jokes and teasing, whistles and catcalls of various kinds. Non-verbal harassment: suggestive gestures or looks, winking and indecent licking of the lips, and the display of placards, photographs, or drawings of a sexual nature. Physical harassment: rape or attempted rape, pressing another person into a corner or against a wall, pinching, shoving or slapping, as well as touching, embracing, and kissing.

The explanations that define the distinctions are not altogether clear to me. My guidelines define verbal harassment in ways that confuse me. It may be harassment, the pamphlet says, if someone insists on getting together even after you've said "no." It might not be sexual harassment if someone asks you out and accepts your "no." Non-verbal harassment confuses me, too. It may be sexual harassment, say the guidelines, if a person stares often at your body, but the behavior probably is not sexual harassment if the person stares at you as you walk by. As far as physical harassment is concerned, the situation is much clearer. The difference lies in frequency. My guidelines state that if someone regularly rubs up against us that is physical harassment, but it is probably not if the same or another person bumps into us in passing.

This sexual harassment is a dangerous thing because it can take a variety of forms, say my guidelines. So I am constantly on guard. For instance, I don't want sexual harassment to affect my working ability. Certainly not. The instructive sketch that moves me most is a picture of a woman worker wearing a protective helmet. And while in the bubble above her head there is a clock with wings, i.e., she is thinking of the way time is flying by, meanwhile, above the head of her colleague, also in a helmet, is a bubble with very different thoughts: a table for two at a restaurant! If I were ever to meet such a man wearing a protective helmet with fantasies about restaurants above his head, and if he were to start insisting I go out with him, if he kept plying me with presents and making offensive comments about my appearance and clothes (especially if we bear in mind that I'm wearing a helmet!), if he touches me in a way I find disagreeable (rather than agreeable), if he tells me sexy jokes and keeps hanging up posters with sexual messages in my vicinity, I have the right to take the creep straight to court. This is what my guidelines guarantee.

I notice that I avoid looking at a person I'm talking to for longer than three seconds. I keep lowering my eyes. I'm becoming paranoid. I don't lick my lips even when I'm eating pancakes with maple syrup, my favorite American treat. I don't, after all, know how people around me would interpret lip-licking. I have become alert to every kind of physical abuse. I don't invite anyone to my place. I don't accept invitations. You never know. Harassment may be lying in wait for you around any corner.

This is one of the reasons why I like New York. I can secretly live out my desires there. I go into the crowded subway, mingle with unknown bodies, I enjoy all the jostling. I especially like the subway on rainy days: I like mingling with anonymous coats damp with rain. I let my gaze roam freely over the faces, I carry out clandestine harassment. On the escalators I wink at one person, blow an air kiss to another. My kiss floats upward or downward and lands on someone like a soft little feather. I adore New York crowds, my shoulder bumps someone, someone else bumps me, I touch someone in passing, I collect touches like matchsticks. So as not to be too cold in Middletown.

Because I do feel cold in Middletown. Smaller places are more conscientious about following the rules of behavior. As I walk along Court Street, I see a mother out for a walk with her little son. They are enjoying the cold, sunny day. I look at the boy's pale profile, there's something touching about him.

"What's your name, buddy?" I ask, in a friendly way.

"I don't talk to strangers," says the boy looking solemnly straight ahead.

"Really," I say.

"I don't talk to strangers," repeats the child, looking straight ahead.

"Why?" I say.

"I don't talk to strangers," repeats the child persistently.

"I'm sorry, ma'am," his mother joins in solemnly, "please don't talk to him. I've taught him not to talk to anyone he doesn't know. Too many horrible things are happening, you know."

"I understand, so sorry," I wince and hurry away.

So ready to find in every little thing a universal, obsessive topic, to dissect it collectively, to take it to its extreme conclusion, extreme instances, to articulate and define it, to institutionalize it—whether it is D-Day, catastrophes, jaws, earthquakes, parasites, cancerous rays, unicorns, or AIDS—Americans are currently obsessed with sexual harassment and the sexual abuse of children.

It seems to me, a foreigner forgetting for a moment where I'm from, that America is living through all the myths of all the cultures that came into being before her; that she is experiencing them passionately, collectively, in a fairy tale, ignorant mish-mash, where the origin quoted is not important, what matters is the story. It seems to me that in America any theme that has the structure of myth, a primordial form, a fairy tale, an archetype, tends to take hold. Myth is a fable, American culture is fabulistic. American culture is profoundly mythic. So it is not at all clear (or important) whether the theme of sexual harassment has been brought to the surface by genuine and, as they say, alarming statistics, or whether it is just the infantile longing of collective America for a new myth, a new collective psychoanalytical theme. Or both. Such a theme is readily taken up by the media, the newspapers, publishing houses, television, the movie industry, it becomes a public, collective, and personal nightmare, it informs behavior, attitudes, it sparks new laws, like adrenaline it quickens the collective American metabolism, sharpens the sensibilities, clarifies attitudes.

But if I, a foreigner, remember for a moment where I'm from, I'm suddenly chastened, and then I feel that America is profoundly right. The history of the Balkan countries, after all, is nothing but a history of mutual harassment. "This nation has suffered too much," writes Ivo Andrić, "from disorder, violence, and injustice and is too used to bearing them with a muffled grumble, or else rising up against them, according to the times and circumstances. Our people's lives pass, bitter and empty, among malicious, vengeful thoughts and periodic revolts. To anything else, they are insensitive and inaccessible. One sometimes wonders whether the spirit of the majority of the Balkan peoples has not forever been poisoned and that, perhaps, they will never again be able to do anything other than suffer violence, or inflict it."

I don't care right now whether Andrić was being fair or not, just as I don't care whether I, myself, am perpetuating the stereotypes about the Balkans and the "Balkan curse." My guilt is negligible. The tale of "Balkan doom" is being earnestly inflated by the local murderers and butchers, not the writers. What worries me, however, is something else. I am aghast at the thought that my momentary scornful arrogance might be of the same ilk as the malevolence with which my agile compatriots are destroying their country. And so, yes, you're right, ma'am. Teach your child not to talk to strangers, you're right, too many horrible things are happening in the world . . .

EEWs

I ENVY "WESTERN" writers. I see my colleague, a Western writer, as an elegant passenger traveling with no luggage. I see myself as a passenger traveling with an enormous load of luggage, a passenger trying desperately to shed his burden, but dragging it tenaciously after him like destiny itself.

My Zagreb dentist with "a natural talent for inflicting pain" asked me several months ago what I was doing in his clinic, meaning, why I was not off at the front.

"Sorry?"

"You're a writer, aren't you?"

"Apparently."

"Then you ought to be at the front. To learn what blood looks like!"

"I'm squeamish at the sight of blood."

"Squeamish? At a time when people are dying for our homeland you sit here calmly having your cavities filled and dare to say you're squeamish at the sight of blood!" barked my Zagreb dentist, angrily brandishing his drill over my head.

It was several months ago in the dentist's chair that it first occurred to me that all my life I had been doing everything in my power to cling to my right to my one single privilege. The privilege of being a writer. I refused to be a member of political parties, organizations, commissions, juries, I avoided being left or right, above or below. I was an accursed outsider. I refused membership in mountaineering, feminist, or diving clubs. I believed a writer should have no homeland or nation or nationality, a writer must serve neither Institution nor Nation, neither God nor the Devil, a writer must have only one identity: his books, I thought, and only one homeland: Literature (where did I get that idea?).

Alarmed by so powerful an argument as the dentist's drill, I admitted that the dentist was right and left the country. If I could do nothing for my homeland, I thought, at least I could preserve my right to freedom, I would fight for the right to preserve my writing from serving anyone or anything but itself. My Literature, my Belles Lettres, I repeated to myself, clutching my only ID, my books, in hand . . .

As soon as I crossed the border, the customs officers of culture began crudely attaching identity labels to me: *communism*, *Eastern Europe*, *censorship*, *repression*, *Iron Curtain*, *nationalism* (Serb or Croat?)—the very labels from which I'd succeeded in protecting my writing in my own country.

"What do you think of communism?" an American journalist asked me. "I'm sure it was terrible," she said grimacing with emotion. "But in a transitional period the phenomenon itself seeks rearticulation . . ."

I listened to her, and I couldn't believe my ears. How could she know it was *terrible*, and how easily all those words: communism, transition, post-communism tripped off her tongue.

"I'm not a politician, I'm a writer," I said.

"I'm asking you because you're a writer, an intellectual, the representative of a post-communist country . . ."

God, I thought, if she only knew that in my country there were writers who had assumed the role of politicians, who were as responsible for the war as were the generals, because when asked these same questions they were only too eager to answer.

"We're talking about literature," I said.

"Let's leave the boring questions about literature to the Western writers. As an East European writer and intellectual you surely have far more interesting things to talk about than literature."

At gatherings here I sometimes come across colleagues of mine, "Easterners," EEWs (East European Writers), and see how they've adapted in advance to the given stereotype, how readily they chatter on about censorship (though they've had no experience of it themselves). I hear them prattle on about post-communism, about the everyday life of their sad Eastern Europe, talking about democracy in transition, proposing measures for moving beyond the crisis (from nationalism to agriculture!), eagerly embracing the identity tags, wearing them like badges, sticking together—the Russians with the Hungarians, Hungarians with Czechs, Czechs with Poles, Poles with Romanians, Romanians with Bulgarians—as though they all wanted to pull that enormous, intriguing post-communist turnip out of the ground together.

I sometimes come across my compatriots here as well, and watch them go on about ex-Yugoslavia, the war and its causes (having escaped from both the war and its causes!), making personal statements, becoming *the voice of the people*, accepting the role they escaped at home and are now glad to take upon themselves; I watch them adapting, modeling their own biographies, no longer knowing how much is true and what is a newly acquired image. I look at my colleagues, those sweaty travelers wrestling with their luggage: with several suitcases already in hand, I can see on their faces their readiness to take on more.

"The American market is saturated with East European writers," said an editor in one publishing house.
"Oh?" I said.
"I personally don't intend to publish a single one," he said.
"But what has that got to do with my books?" I said, stressing the word "books."
"You are an East European writer," he replied, stressing every word.

"It's a real shame you're not a Cuban writer," said the editor of another publishing house, with feeling.
"Oh?"
"The American market is receptive to ethnicities at the moment, particularly Cubans, Puerto Ricans, Latin America in general."
"Interesting," I said.
"Do you have any connection to China?"
"No."
"Pity. That would have helped too. The Chinese immigrant novel, that's in fashion at the moment."

"Unfortunately we can't publish your books just now," said the editor of a third publishing house, with a real note of regret. "You write, how can I put it, 'literary' literature. From a moral standpoint it would not be right to publish something like that now that your country is at war. Have you written anything about the war?"
"I'm squeamish at the sight of blood," I said and remembered I'd uttered the very same words several months before.
"I'm sorry, really sorry," said the editor sincerely.
"But what do you have to do with the war in Yugoslavia?" I asked.

"To publish anything else at this moment would mean that as a publishing house we are indifferent to the political events in the world," said the editor with conviction.

Here in America, clutching my books, my one and only ID, I am aware of all the tragi-comedy of EEWs, the labeled East European Writers, dragging their wretched homelands around with them as necessary baggage, never having been saddled with them until they came here, of course. Along the way I feel like a kind of female Don Quixote who still cares about Belles Lettres at a time when it is changing its appearance, when things are being measured by labels and not content, at a time when Literature is hidden under the names of its producers. Armani, Eco, Toshiba . . .

At a party I'm approached by a smooth-shaven man twisting a glass around by the stem. I recognize the face of an American publisher.
"I'm told you're a writer," he smiles.
And I feel myself jettisoning my whole burden as the labels unstick and peel off. I draw myself up elegantly and say:
"You're mistaken. I'm a typist."
"Oh?" says the publisher with a smile and moves away, twisting his glass in his fingers.
Somewhere in a corner, my Literature smiles gratefully, my invisible Belles Lettres. And, raising my glass, I smile back.

Personality

I CALL AN acquaintance, a New Yorker, I haven't seen her for three years. "Oh, great to hear from you! How are you?" "And how are you?" . . . We chat, we condense three years of our lives into brief reports: she's finished her doctorate and found a job and had a daughter. "Oh, you must come and see her! She has such a strong personality." This footnote—strong personality—pricks my ear like an acupuncture needle and won't go away.

I imagine a spoiled brat, which is what "strong personality" means in this case. The brat part doesn't bother me, it's the intonation. Because she, my acquaintance, doesn't know I've heard this phrase, spoken with that same intonation, countless times since I've been here, and that suggests to me that there is a predominance here of people with strong personalities, so, therefore, my life here was going to be remarkably exciting.

There's an entire industry for the production of personality. Child psychologists, adult psychiatrists, laws, established codes of behavior, newspapers, publishing houses, television. Everything is for sale, from textbooks with ego-building exercises to audiocassettes advising us how to turn a grating voice into one that is deep and agreeable.

But still, in order for a person to have a personality, he must, it would seem, earn it, he has to have a destiny that will be authentic and his alone. But the praxis of everyday life rudely quashes one's right to a personal destiny simply because it instantly transforms it into a public, collective one.

In totalitarian systems the individual preserved his privacy like the family valuables. What he did not himself succeed in preserving in the "house safe," was preserved in police safes—by the police. The police were as discreet as one's most loyal friend. The genre of the personal confession is unknown to the literatures of totalitarian systems (the less you talk about yourself, the thinner your police file will be!). Indeed, literature begins where the personal confession ends. Literature under totalitarian regimes has exploited the rich strategies of literary devices, lies—the essence of literature, in other words—in order to express its truth indirectly about the world. With the fall of communism, the genre of the personal confession sprang into being: suddenly it transpired that our lives were like two peas in a pod. The freedom of confession has destroyed the aura of uniqueness the author used to have, the aura of tragic personal fate.

It seems that America does not produce anything other than the genre of collective autobiography. The average American appears to be lurching unconsciously toward a large media interviewing room where they will confess their lives. The role of the discreet police in totalitarian systems has been taken over in the American democratic system by the indiscreet media. Bookstores are full of personal stories that describe the author (he or she) being raped, surviving incurable disease, curing depression, dragging themselves out of the jaws of drug addiction, doing this and doing that.

American television programs, too, have become public collective confessionals: they compete as to who will confess more, better, more keenly. TV confessionals are like gladiators' arenas in which the fighters wrestle with emotions, and the audience enjoys the fresh, authentic bloodletting. Confessions are sometimes produced like real Greek plays: relations, sisters, brothers, and children are brought on to play out an authentic family melodrama before the eyes of the viewers. Americans today make public confessions of their personal experience—to order.

And what has happened to the sacred American right to privacy?

If you stare at an American's house for longer than three minutes, the owner has the right, according to one of the many laws that sanction the sacred right to privacy, to call the police. On the other hand this same American will not hold back from telling you his whole life story at the first available opportunity. If he holds back, the media will do it for him. Because the private is public. It is not advisable in America today to shut the door of the office where you work. During office hours professors keep their doors wide open so as not to be accused of harassment. And the right to personal illness has also been withdrawn. This is why Magic Johnson briefly informed the media as he emerged from the delivery room: "He's negative!" The whole of America knew what this "negative" referred to. Johnson's newborn baby did not have HIV! Even the right to personal suicide has been withdrawn, as the very next day the media will make your tragic, fresh, personal corpse into a collective sociological theme.

America today is writing its great collective autobiography. And when everyone writes, what ensues is a universal deafness and lack of understanding, as Kundera once wrote. The American market of ideas is not giving up, the commercial effect of the personal obliges it to establish new aesthetic criteria: only what is *truthful*, *authentic*, *personal* is of aesthetic value.

Will Americans soon begin to wonder how it is that they—who have believed their whole lives in ideologemes about individualism, individual choice, personalness—are so remarkably like their next-door neighbors? The American media market, which anticipates all problems by immediately giving them voice, offers its new, great, global, safeguarding idea of self-esteem. Work on self-esteem (national, professional, age-specific, physical, private, sexual) anticipates the awareness of defeat, the awareness that something isn't quite right after all—because this implies in advance that something is wrong. Work on self-esteem is a form of ego-training as a safeguard, a new fashion product on the American market of ideas.

And if I change the lens for a moment and ask myself who I am, the observer, I'm acutely aware that my self-esteem suddenly melts away. Have the sick the right to judge the healthy? Am I not a sort of invalid observing the reality around me from a wheelchair with the eyes of a limited and therefore superficial observer?

What is the state of my personal "me"? Have I ever asked myself that? Have I ever wondered how much I am the product of many years of the fine crocheting of the system in which I lived, and how much I am myself? And am I not at this moment NO ONE, just a number with no identity, am I not anonymous human flesh in the hands of the warlords? Because they, the warlords, in my name, without consulting me, are deciding in what state I am to live, in which language I am to write, to which culture I will belong, they are deciding whether they will grant or take away the life of those close to me, of my friends, whether they will destroy my towns, they are deciding the names of my streets, erasing my past, determining my present, sketching my future, altering my personal documents, deciding whether they will stop me from meeting my friends or allow me to see them in what was until a short time ago our shared country, they decide whether and where I'll travel, where the new borders of the state I am to live in will be, which newspapers I'll read, where I can and where I cannot call by phone, they decide what will be truth and what a lie, they decide whom I'll love and whom I'll hate, which words I'll in the future be permitted to use and which not. Even my decision to leave the country will not be my own, personal decision, because they will have driven me to it, not even a decision to kill myself would be my personal choice, because they would have forced it on me. So, what am I, the arrogant observer, what is the state of my personal me and what about my self-esteem? And what gives me the right, from my refugee's disjointed, neurotic, desperate, and disabled standpoint, to judge a world that is freely setting up its norms, the norms of its normalcy?

I'm sitting on a bench in Central Park. It's Sunday, it's sunny, I light a cigarette, I smile the smile of a convalescent and watch amazed as Americans run, walk, roller-skate, take their children, their dogs, their bodies, their personalities for a walk. A woman with headphones on her ears, and a little cassette-player hooked onto her belt, comes running toward me in a tight, shiny jogging suit. She notices me and her face twists into a sudden grimace of anger.

"You're polluting our park," she shouts.

I immediately stub out my personal cigarette. She runs on, joins another jogger, then they both join a third. I watch the three of them moving harmoniously and personally away, running off into some collective future. The rays of the sun, glinting off the metal headphones on their heads and gleaming like an aura, simply reinforce that impression.

Melancholy

1.

Ellen calls. She apologizes for calling so early, she wanted to see whether we're still on for the concert that evening.
"Sure, and why wouldn't we be?"
"Well, I just wanted to see."
"What time is it?"
"Six."
"And you're calling me for that at six o'clock in the morning?"
"Sorry . . ."

Ellen explained everything. "I'm fond of you," she said, "and first thing as soon as I wake up I call all the people I care about. And I get up early, what can you do, nerves. But if I don't call and don't check whether you are all where you should be, I can't start my day. I have to," said Ellen. "Otherwise I'm afraid people might disappear. Sometimes I'm scared I no longer exist."

I understand Ellen completely. She is Jewish and from New York City; she has a long family history of disappearance. And she herself has experienced some of it. First her mother died, then her father, then her first husband, and then lawyers had their way with her last refuge, her parents' apartment with a view of Central Park. And so it was that Ellen, at the age of fifty-three, found herself on the street with three children—though the kids were grown—with two doctorates in hand and less than two years of work experience, a few published books, and scholarly standing in psychoanalytic circles. Her children were, fortunately, near the end of their studies, so they'd manage. Ellen is an intellectual nomad, facing penury. She totes her property around with her in her car: her computer, some clothing, and a few family photographs. One way or another, she makes ends meet, a stipend here, a short-term teaching position for a semester or two there.

2.

I have no God of my own, so I have no church, which doesn't mean that there aren't moments when I am in need of consolation. When I find myself seeking comfort, I go to the closest place, to Woolworths.

At Woolworths, or at least the one in my neighborhood, large black women come to do their shopping. The women move with a whale's grace, slowly and serenely they turn things over in their hands, they do their shopping with care. The slow-motion movements of the customers (who are large black women) and the saleswomen (who are large black women) have a soothing effect on me. Woolworths is for buying smaller items, a pair of socks, a plastic hairbrush, an inexpensive frying pan, hair dye, a synthetic bra, a little comfort, a momentary feeling of belonging to a class, a race, or a group that is or feels to be ours.

Woolworths, like many other institutions (even many places of worship) is a place marked by class. A limousine with tinted windows never pulls up in front of Woolworths, the Woolworths customers go there on foot. Woolworths has the air of a museum, it is a swaybacked old merchant nag breathing its last, a realm for consumer melancholy. The products sold here pledge a faith in a better and happier future. This is a "future" that was achieved some time ago. This is why Woolworths products evoke a furtive sense of melancholy among the more sensitive customers. A faith in the future of plastic, synthetic, and nylon has been preserved at Woolworths. And plastic, synthetic, and nylon are the America of my childhood, the childhood of America itself. Woolworths is a stand-in for the flea market, a burial ground for the consumer utopia, a dream of middle-class happiness. Synthetic, plastic, and nylon are today the symbolic proletarian fist shaken helplessly at the luxury of cotton and linen. For the utopia of synthetics has meanwhile become the reality of the poor. Woolworths is a place of retro-utopia, it has a whiff of resignation and extinction, which must be what attracts me to it.

3.

Seventeen years ago, when I was in Moscow for a year as a student, I traveled with a student group around Georgia, Armenia, and Uzbekistan. In Erevan, having left our things at the hotel, four of us women from Sweden, the Netherlands, the United States, and I left the group and set off to tour the city. Among ourselves we were speaking Russian, we were young and confident. Confidence comes with youth, but it also came from the fact that we were in a country where life was much harder than the life we'd known. We couldn't have understood this then, that our self-confidence sprang from simple things such as a reliable passport and credit cards.

A young man stopped us on the street. He was polite and asked if we had jeans to sell. At the time jeans were the Eastern European mantra. We told him we didn't, but the young man didn't blink an eye, as if the jeans didn't interest him much anyway. He asked me if I'd go out with him in the evening. I agreed without a second thought, probably because it never occurred to me that I'd be going out with someone I knew nothing about. And besides, we'd already said that all of us together, our whole student group, would be going out in the evening.

It turned out I'd misremembered something and missed hearing where the group had agreed to congregate. None of "my" people were left at the hotel, and then I remembered the young man. Better to go out, I thought, than to sit alone in the hotel room.

He was waiting for me in the hotel lobby. He wasn't alone, he'd come with a friend. We got into a car waiting out in front of the hotel, driven by his friend.
"He is a well-known Armenian boxer," said the young man with pride. I wasn't listening. I was reeling in a sudden panic. How stupid could I be, I thought, I'm not just going out with boys I don't know, but one of them's a boxer! As we drove farther out of town, the streets were darker. The young men chatted. Frozen with this panic, I couldn't utter a word. The car stopped in front of a house, the boys led me up some narrow, worn steps. When the boy rang the doorbell, I froze in terror; there, now they'd rob me, rape me, murder me, and nobody would ever find me again.

The door opened. A kind gray-haired woman greeted us at the door. "Do come in," she said to me, "we are so pleased you agreed to visit us," she said, "foreigners, you know we so seldom have the opportunity to welcome you to our home."

The boy's mother brought us into the kitchen where a festive table had been set. The boy's older brother was sitting at the table. The boxer apologized politely that he wouldn't be able to stay for dinner. My feeling of panic was replaced by shame. Again I chastised myself: God, how unimaginative I am, how foolishly paranoid.

The gray-haired woman sat at the head of the table, the food was delicious, the boy was courteous and friendly. Only the boy's older brother (he might have been around forty) was a little absent and odd. After dinner the lady of the house showed me her family picture album and talked about her family, her husband who'd died, and her sons. I was muddled, I was still anguished by guilt at my suspicions. Now I was beginning to be uncomfortable at the kindness my hosts were so generous with.

Then at one moment the older brother mumbled something about showing me his room. The room was like a magpie's nest. It was a little household altar celebrating the Goddess America, a grotesque temple of a wretched collector, the obsessive fantasy of a madman. Some of the things had been cadged from the rare American tourist, some of it had been collected for years from the newspapers, some of it had turned up by chance. On the walls hung the Kennedys and posters, photographs of film stars, many postcards with American images, miniature American flags (the sort used to decorate cakes and sandwiches), heaps of Coca-Cola cans and bottles, key rings with a picture of John F. Kennedy, American trinkets, trash, and kitsch lined shelves, as if on an altar.

"You aren't American, are you."
"No, I'm not."
"Have you ever been to America?" he asked.
"No, I haven't."

"America's the best! Isn't it the best? I adore everything American. What about you? . . . Here we're living in shit! This is all shit! If only I could only get away from here . . . Leave . . . See America . . ." the crazed man mumbled.

The woman was standing at the door. She nodded to me and I slipped out, leaving the man to his mumbles.

"He's not well, you can see for yourself that he's not well . . ." she whispered.

A little later I said my goodbyes and the woman embraced me warmly as I left. The boy offered to see me back to the hotel.

"You saw my brother . . . You're a student, you're living in Moscow, you must have a lot of friends . . . Surely you know an American woman . . . I was thinking, maybe one of them might be willing to marry my brother . . . An arrangement. We'd pay. You have no idea how obsessed he is with America," said the boy in a breath.

My heart sank. Now I understood all of it. The boy had invited me home because I was a foreigner. To be a foreigner in the Soviet Union at that time was a value in and of itself, sufficient reason to invite someone in off the street. The boy was too young to be able to recognize the accents and he knew the geographic and political priorities. Every foreigner might just be an American.

I imagined how after our morning encounter on the street the boy had raced home, breathless, talked his mother into making dinner, found a friend with a car so the "foreigner" wouldn't be troubled by the walk. They showed the very best they had in their modest apartment and that was it: the Armenian dinner and the family picture album. At dinner they'd realized I wasn't American. They didn't suggest in any way that such a thing mattered to them. Indeed the woman said a few kind words about Yugoslavia. And now, at the end, the boy was trying desperately to salvage his childish project.

At the entrance to the hotel I extended my hand to shake his. By his clasp I could tell that he was younger than he looked, a child who'd assumed the role of father and concern for his crazy brother.

"You won't forget, you'll ask around?"

"I won't forget, I'll ask around."

I left him out in front of the hotel. The slip of paper with his address I threw away. The next day we left for Tashkent.

4.

I have no idea how to explain what moved me to bring together here things that are essentially so unlike: the student episode of years ago, the Woolworths in my neighborhood, and Ellen. The only bond among them is the sadness they stir in me now, a melancholy arising from unrequited human longing, as well from when these are met.

I should say that since I've come to know Ellen I've developed a compulsive neurotic disorder. I call people I care about to see if they are where they should be. Ellen knows that the world is more fragile than we realize, things disappear, countries disappear, people disappear, a brief moment of inattention is all that's needed for the world around us to cease, suddenly, to be ours.

If I wake up too early, and if I'm overcome by qualms about disappearing and haven't the heart to bother my nearest and dearest to check and see whether they are all where they should be, I dial the number of the federal Internal Revenue Service for instant consolation. A human being almost never picks up, but they play Aram Khachaturian's "Dance with Swords," and though it may not be overly persuasive, at least it provides audible proof that the world is still where it should be.

Ellen called me this morning.
"I've been hired to teach in San Francisco!"
"Cheers . . ." I mumble groggily.
"Now at least I'll be able to call my New York friends without guilt."
"How so?"
"The three-hour time difference!" said Ellen sweetly. "When I get up it will be nine o'clock New York time . . ."

Contact

Some ten years ago I was in New Orleans. I was there with Judis and Hans, writers. The excursion to New Orleans had been organized for us by the Iowa City Writers' Workshop, as we were their guests. At the airport we were met by a strong, handsome man missing a hand, who introduced himself as Chris. He drove us to our hotel and promised to come for us in the evening.

At that point I didn't know that the strong, handsome man was one of thousands of volunteers, members of societies of lovers of contact with foreigners, or something like that. He came to our hotel and took us out to dinner. During the meal we discovered that Chris was a social worker. After dinner he divided the bill neatly into four. Then Chris took out a thick notebook whose pages were covered with the signatures of people from all over the world. They had signed their names and added something about "the unforgettable evening" or about "Chris's hospitality in New Orleans." And we, too, duly signed. "I have contacts throughout the world, 155 names to be precise," said Chris. Then he took us back to the hotel, where we exchanged business cards. Later I received a postcard from New Orleans with greetings from Chris. That was all. Sometimes I think of that strong, handsome man without a hand. I wonder how many more names he has collected in his notebook, and whether there's any deeper meaning to his sad collection and the whole episode.

Some time ago I attended a literary conference. Afterward my American friend Norman called me and asked, excited, "Did you make any contacts?"
Norman preferred the sacred word *contact* to such words as: intellectual stimulus, exchange of ideas, friendship, acquaintance, meaningful encounter. Or was all of this implied by the metallic-tasting word "contact"?

In Middletown I was invited by the friendly president of the Exchange Club to give a lecture at one of the club's meetings about "the current dramatic events in Yugoslavia." The president kept calling; the secretary assured me that none of the visiting lecturers had yet refused Exchange—and I relented. On the appointed day a colleague took me to a nearby restaurant where the meetings of Exchange, a club of Middletown businessmen, are held. After their meeting I was asked to say a few words and I stood at the improvised rostrum, sweating and blushing at the absolute pointlessness of the situation. It was crystal clear that the members of the Exchange Club neither knew the whereabouts of the country I was describing, nor, in fact, were they interested, and it was more than obvious that I should not be spoiling their lunch with stories about other people's corpses. Out of courtesy they asked a few questions, I answered briefly, then the waiters brought the food, and then the president came to the rostrum and gave me a ballpoint pen with the word "Exchange" inscribed on it. The businessmen clapped and we ate the warm sandwiches. Later, at home, I stared at my honorarium, the ballpoint pen, and wept. Chewing over my twinge of insult, I wondered whether there was any deeper meaning at all to this pointless episode.

One Sunday Norman invited me to visit some old friends of his. "It will be wonderful," he said, "Steven will be coming from New York and Frank from Los Angeles."

We drove for three hours to reach the home of Norman's friends, a lawyer and his wife, a psychologist. New York Steven and LA Frank were already there. The psychologist wife was occupied with a do-it-yourself task: assembling a Shaker chair she'd ordered through a catalogue. The men would occasionally hammer in a nail, discussing whether the firm canvas strips ought to be stretched this way or that. I went out from time to time onto the porch to smoke, because the hosts and their guests, every last one, were allergic to cigarette smoke. Then we sat in the living room (the wife had stopped working on her Shaker chair). Frank, a living museum exhibit from the sixties, trotted out something about global love, sex, meditation, self-esteem, about the book he was in the process of writing. As he did so our hostess stretched herself over a big rubber ball, a new fitness product. She kneaded the ball with her body: first she rolled over the ball on her back, then she sat on the ball with her legs apart and slowly kneaded the muscles of her buttocks, then she lay on her front and thoroughly kneaded her stomach muscles. At the same time she talked to me about the topic of her doctoral dissertation and defended the effectiveness of hypnosis in treating certain psychological disorders. My friend Norman stretched out on the couch, deep in preparation for a lecture for the following day, and then dozed off. Our host was busy with logs and keeping the fire going in the fireplace. As he did so he kindly explained to me which wood burns more quickly and which more slowly.

Beside the fireplace was a manual about making and maintaining fires. From time to time I went out onto the porch to smoke. Dusk gradually gathered. When it was completely dark, Norman woke, LA Frank had finished his lecture about global self-esteem, and someone suggested we should have something to eat. First we had a lengthy discussion as to which cuisine we should choose—Chinese, Indian, Japanese, or Mexican—and then someone decided, because of me, that we should have something "American" so we drove to a nearby diner. In the little restaurant we ate quickly and then parted warmly. "Come again, you really must come again," said my hostess warmly. "Of course," I said, "it was lovely!" In the car, on our way home, I wondered whether this pointless encounter had any deeper meaning. Unlike me, my American friend Norman seemed very pleased. He had been with people and it had not hurt. That was the whole point. When I am with people, my own people, in the end it always hurts.

A little while ago I watched a television program about highly educated immigrants from Eastern Europe. Physicists, mathematicians, doctors, engineers, architects from Bulgaria, Romania, Hungary—they were all attending classes to learn how to find jobs in America. On the blackboard was a message written in large letters: Network Or No Work!

"Contact," "network," "networking" are words that are part of American etiquette, automatic American behavior. Meanwhile the human specimens who work on making and keeping contacts do not wonder about their meaning, but simply behave. They collect business cards in their organizers, jot down addresses, call, write thank-you letters, even when there is no occasion meriting gratitude, take your telephone number but do not call, warmly invite you to a party yet sometimes forgetting to give you the address, fall over themselves to come to your party without forgetting to take your address. In the little dictionary of etiquette, words stick to one another like magnets. The words "contact" and "networking" are joined by another two: "image" and "schedule." It is almost impossible to network without an image or a schedule. Regarding the grand idea of the image, the fundamental notion is that in the world of the media the picture is everything; in the world of pictures, everything is an impression. American socializing ideology offers numerous suggestions as to how to design and redesign your own image, how to create a favorable impression, how to increase your personal social rating. The image is a small step on the path to eternity, to myth.

The schedule is the organizer: the daily, monthly, yearly, or even several-yearly timetable according to which Americans conduct their work, their life and the network of their contacts. Even when dying of boredom, even when there hasn't been a human being on the horizon for days, an American will not leap at the first invitation, but will say: Hmm, let me look at my schedule. Americans are long-lived. It would seems that this is not thanks to widely shared anxiety about health, but to the simple word "schedule." When Death knocks at an American's door, I imagine the American saying: Hmm, let me look at my schedule.

What can I do? I am adapting, doing my level best to contact and network. As far as networks go, I've joined one. I stumbled on it quite by chance by ordering from a catalogue something called "The Magic Ear." What is a "magic ear"? It's a small rubber device with little rubber pins that you insert into your ear in order to inhibit hunger pangs. Ever since the magic ear walked into my life, my mailbox has been full of letters. I have a personal letter from Demis Roussos revealing the *astonishing secret* of how he lost 117 pounds. Miss Ingeborg Bach from Brazil writes that she lost 42 pounds, thanks to Demis's secret. Mrs.

Charrier from France writes that she lost 75 pounds. I am in contact with Mario Tsounio from Greece, Stephanie Presley, Brigitte Barrol, Doctors Hay and Walb . . . I am no longer alone in this (American) world, I am the member of a network of diligent losers of pounds. As for the ear, I have lost or mislaid it somewhere. Or perhaps, using its little rubber needles, it has simply wandered off.

As for contacts, I have made one of these as well. George Fazzino is my driving instructor, my precious American contact.
"Write Fazzina," George corrects me as I write a check after the lesson.
"Why? Isn't your name Fazzino?" I ask.
"In Middletown there are so many Italians called Fazzino that I've decided to call myself Fazzina."
"I understand," I say, changing the "o" to "a."

George is a Vietnam vet and an aging heart-throb. Now George is a family man, he has grown-up children, he's about to become a grandfather. George says he studied psychology. As we cruise around the streets of Middletown and its surroundings a lot of people roll down the windows of their cars to call: "Do you remember me?"
"Of course!" George shouts back warmly, waving. "He must have been a student of mine," George turns to me, a little touched. He thinks of all the pupils he has taught to drive.

Every time we have a lesson George makes me turn from the road into a small gas station. There's a little café there where George and I go for a coffee. George likes the place. The shop changes owners every week. The first owner was Ricardo, an Italian, then Rosy and Mary, and the present owner is a young guy from Pakistan, Amid. Amid is, of course, our new friend. We always talk with Amid about life. We talk to each owner about life. Especially Rosy and Mary. Rosy was only 18 and already pregnant for the second time. Her husband drank and often beat her.

While we're at our café George and I always check the little pond with fish—minnows—because there is nothing there but coffee, newspapers, and minnows. That's why the place keeps changing owners.
"Are there any fish around here?" I ask George.
"Probably," says George.
And we watch contentedly as our minnows dart about.
"No there aren't," says Amid. "If there were any fish, someone would presumably be buying the minnows as bait."
Every time we go to the café George buys a lottery ticket. He scratches the shiny surface of the little ticket with his nail, and what peers out from underneath regularly is—loss.
"Have you ever won anything?"
"Oh yes," says George. "Last year I won $50."

As we drive George and I talk about life: I tell him about my students, about the war in my country. George knows everything, the names of the destroyed cities, the number of casualties, he's angry with Milosevic. "Son of a bi . . ." George has the whole world in his little finger, because he has a student driver from China, a student driver from Uzbekistan, an angry Filippino student driver . . . George is knowledgeable about my literary problems as well, he discusses genres with me, the role of literature in the postmodern age and postmodernism altogether . . .
"Hmm," George shakes his head anxiously. "Where is contemporary literature heading, I'd like to know."

We park outside my house after every lesson. Parking is not my strong point, I brake too suddenly, and my braking sends various odds and ends flying at us. George's car is full of free cosmetic samples, trinkets, little bottles of perfume, makeup bags. This is George's other job, he is a traveling salesman. He gallantly gives me a little something each time we meet. Last time I was given a whole assortment of headache pills.

Last time a book fell on us, too, a 150-year-old Italian book of dreams that had belonged to George's father, Silvestro. Friends visit George, tell him their dreams, George checks the meaning of their dreams in his dream book—every dream has a number—and tells his friends the numbers. His friends buy lottery tickets using those numbers and they always win.
"What about you?" I ask George.
"It doesn't work for me. I've tried so many times, but it doesn't work . . . I'm jinxed!"

Recently George confided in me his greatest secret. He's about to go into the production of cubes of frozen lemonade. The lemonade recipe is a secret, the secret has been passed down from generation to generation in the Fazzino family, or at least ever since there have been ice and lemonade. George and I spent a long time discussing the name of the product, and eventually decided on "Sylvester."
"That would be right, after all," said George with emotion.
I have no doubt that the magic of the late Silvestro will work in the end and that George will ultimately grow rich. In any case, for some time I have been calling ice cubes, though only ordinary ones, "fazzinis." It makes the ice cubes in my glass melt more quickly and cheerfully.

Recently my American friend Norman called me and, anxious as to my future academic career, asked me:
"Did you make any contacts?"
"Oh, yes! Professor Fazzina," I said mysteriously.

"Fantastic! Hold on to that contact, now, and don't miss out on future ones," he said.

As for my driving, I took the test a while ago. I failed. "Son of a bi . . ." said my instructor George about the examiner who failed me. And he was right.

Comforter

When I heard the air-raid siren in September last year, I didn't realize at first what it meant. My neighbors, unlike me, had memorized the rules for air-raid warnings duly displayed on the elevator door, and they knew at once that this was an air raid. I let my neighbors run down to the cellar, while I, suspicious of all mass phenomena, went back to my apartment. I can no longer remember what I was thinking. Probably nothing. I waited for the alarm to pass. The next day there was another warning, I sat at my desk, and as I listened to the panic-stricken wailing of the siren I wondered what I should take down with me. In the meantime the alarm passed. I consulted my friends about what to take with me to the shelter. My friend Nenad's mother remembered that during the Second World War and the first air-raid warnings in Zagreb, she'd taken her alarm clock down. Why an alarm clock? She couldn't say. But since the alarm clock was the first thing she'd grabbed in her panic, she went on carrying it throughout the air-raid alerts. She survived the war and gave birth to my friend Nenad. What happened to the alarm clock? I didn't ask.

Over the next few days, at every warning siren, I went dutifully down to the cellar in our apartment building. I observed my neighbors. Each time they brought some new item: a blanket (in case it was cold), cushions (to be more comfortable), spades and pickaxes (in case we were buried under rubble), flashlights (in case the electricity went out), radios (to hear the news). Gradually my neighbors progressed from strictly functional items to sprucing up the cellar. They cleaned the firewood bins (arranging them like grotesque, post-apocalyptic replicas of their apartments), they brought playing cards, a book or two, someone brought a comfy armchair, someone a chess set, someone something to drink. Homes, temporarily lost on the upper floors, began to spring up with unbelievable speed in the cellar, in the firewood bins. The ant-like activity in the cellar during the alerts seemed to blunt or defer the clear, sharp thought: so what if the city really were bombed? Wouldn't this all be pointless, then? The books, the belongings, the armchair we spent days over to pick the right color, and the pictures on the walls. That savage thought moved like a cursor erasing row after row, stopping finally at the picture of one's own body: the naked, helpless body clutching its identity card with name, surname, and registration number.

I bought my first computer a few years ago. Thrilled, I wrote my first page and then, undoubtedly due to a mistake, all the sentences I'd written vanished from the screen and all that was left in the center (smack dab in the center!) was the little pronoun I. The tiny letter trembling on the empty screen, which might disappear at any moment—were I accidentally or deliberately to press delete—frightened me, it filled me with sudden dread. I stared petrified at the screen, I felt I was seeing myself on the screen from a terrible distance or terrible proximity. And as if I were nothing more than a personal pronoun, a single trembling letter "I." I sat there for a long time, holding my breath as I watched beating in the middle of the empty screen my fragile, tiny heart.

Several air-raid warnings, several dashes to the shelter with the essentials (I never was able to determine exactly what was most essential) deleted the notion of home for me. An enduring virus of homelessness hacked my system. And it didn't matter whether or not I'd actually lost the roof over my head. My brain registered the sound of the siren, the picture of thousands of refugees (I could have been one), demolished buildings (one of them could have been, and still could be, mine) and it was all stored forever in my memory. My sense of permanent homelessness has been confirmed by my subconscious that now keeps playing games of building a phantom home, which just goes to show how resilient that idea was in me. Or how much more resilient than I thought.

Here in America you don't buy fruit and vegetables by the pound, but by the piece. After a few months I chanced to notice that I always bought four of everything here: four apples, four tomatoes, four grapefruits, four bananas . . . I wondered why four? Why not one, or five, why not three? Then I realized that the number four had been chosen by my subconscious: one apple was for me, the other three were for those closest to me, the three of them. My subconscious had correctly set the default at four.

It is only now, some months later, that I discovered that, although I came here with hardly a single belonging, I see I'll have to buy a new suitcase! The first thing I bought was a comforter. "Comforter" is one of the most common words (or at least I keep stumbling over it); but "comforter" is more than just any old word, a comforter is a status symbol, the cheapest comforters are made of synthetic material and the most expensive of the finest goose down. I borrowed some money and bought the most expensive one straight away. I needed warm winter shoes and a winter coat, but I didn't buy those. I bought what I didn't need. A comforter. What is a comforter? A comforter is a feather bed, a duvet, warm bedding stuffed with feathers. Now I know that this thing, my comforter, was a symbolic substitute for my lost home; my subconscious had infallibly selected an item to serve as a mental roof over my head, a protective shield, a snail's house, a tortoise's shell, an umbrella, a burrow, a hollow, a home.

This is not the whole truth about me. I've held something back. I skipped over mention of the sleeping bag (cotton) and the button-up sack that can be used as a coverlet, a wrap, or a cloak, depending on how you button it up. The idea that someone might see the things I've acquired fills me with horror, I'm already blushing with shame.

I once had a friend who dreamed all his life of the perfect trunk. My friend B. imagined using this trunk for all the things he needed in his life. B. dreamed about the trunk, about an ideal mobile home, in his mind he arranged the things in it carefully, adjusted the compartments, drew new ones in the air. The idea of the ideal trunk possessed him, it was a metaphor for his nightmare, his deep-seated feeling of lacking a home. B. owned both an apartment and a house, but just as in the nightmare, he abandoned the house and apartment, bought or searched for new ones, and somehow even there found no place for himself yet again. At the end of every year I secretly wish for all my friends and acquaintances to live at last in peace with themselves. I wish for B. that he'll find his perfect trunk.

I don't know why it is, but I can no longer remember my favorite books. As soon as I've read a book I forget it. One of my favorites is the novel *Envy* by Yuri Olesha. Sometimes it occurs to me that books are a little like physical pleasure. If we could really remember physical pleasure, we probably wouldn't need to repeat it. It seems we keep repeating "those comic movements" so we can remember pleasure. And then, immediately afterward, someone erases it from our memory and we no longer know what it was like. Delete. It is only the books that give me pleasure that I forget. Nearly all of them. I retain a hazy memory of individual episodes, but I absolutely can't recall what the book was really like.

Ivan Babičev, the hero of Olesha's novel, stands with a pillow tucked under his arm. I stand with my American comforter. A *podushka* and a comforter. We stand, he with his pillow, I with my comforter, and we smile at one another.

We'll all meet up in the heavens, each with our own item. Then we'll know for sure which one thing to take with us into the eternal shelter. Or it will set off of its own accord with us. We'll all be mixed up there, all of us, both those who once lived and those who never lived. Nenad's mother with her alarm clock and Desdemona with her handkerchief. At last we'll know who's who, we'll be naked—each with our own item. We'll read each other's items like a personal biography. There, wrapped in my duvet, I'll meet Ivan Babičev. I'll glance at his pillow and remember the book at last. Every line.

Trash

"Do you think kitsch is a typical product of the communist system?" an American student asked me after a lecture about Kundera's novel *The Unbearable Lightness of Being.*

"Kitsch is a global phenomenon," I said, blushing. I always blush when I make such basic yet trivial statements. At that moment this was, however, the only possible answer. The class was at its end.

In his book about Gogol, Vladimir Nabokov uses the term *poshlost. Poshlost* is a Russian word that, because of its wealth of meanings, Nabokov prefers to English equivalents such as cheap, sham, common, inferior, sorry, trashy, scurvy, tawdry, and the like. By way of illustration of *poshlost* Nabokov takes Gogol's description of a young German gallant. This German is paying court in vain to a young woman who spends every evening sitting on her balcony, knitting stockings and enjoying her view of a lake. Finally the German devises a strategy to capture the young woman's heart. Every evening he undresses, plunges into the lake, and swims before the eyes of his beloved, while at the same time embracing two swans prepared for him especially for that purpose. In the end the young man wins the girl thanks to the water ballet with the swans. While this pure form of *poshlost* merely gives rise to an indulgent smile, another seems to provoke anxiety, one which, as Nabokov says, is "especially vigorous and vicious when the sham is not obvious and when the values it mimics are considered, rightly or wrongly, to belong to the very highest level of art, thought or emotion."

In the schizophrenic minds of the people of the former Yugoslavia, not only are there two realities, past and present, but also two versions of kitsch: the older one and a new one that has sprouted from the old and depends on the recipient consigning the first version to oblivion.

Today, as Yugoslavia falls to pieces (the process is still ongoing even if the governments of the new states have announced and signed its clinical death), in my split consciousness, along with whistling shells, gunfire, screams, wails, laments, and detonations, I hear echoed snatches of folk melodies: Montenegrin, Macedonian, Croatian, Serbian, Albanian. The symbol that has silted into my memory is the circle dance, the "kolo"—performed for years at all state occasions. The kolo was danced by representatives of the ethnic groups of Yugoslavia dressed in their folk costumes. Together they danced all the different dances: they tripped, jigged, skipped, bounced, stamped, twirled as each dance required. The circle dance, the symbolic crown of Yugoslavia, comprehensible to all literate and illiterate Yugoslavs alike, has now become its opposite, a deadly noose. Today, the participants in the Yugoslav kolo are slaughtering one another with the same vigor as they danced, to the sounds of the same fifes and tamburitzas.

The citizen of the former Yugoslavia has not yet forgotten the earlier state kitsch, the monumental performances in which the one and only role was played by the collective body. This body poised, for its president, to line up in the shape of a word, a slogan, a flower, a sumptuous picture on the stadium green. The citizen remembers these spectacles, including the last one, dedicated to Tito. The unnamed socialist designer had dreamed up a swansong: a vast polystyrene sculpture of Tito. Then there was a sudden gust of wind that nearly swept the polystyrene Tito away, and with him the workers who were trying with all their might to stop Tito from flying heavenward.

Just as every tragedy returns as farce, so all the former Yugo-symbols have returned, but now signify the opposite: the baton that used to pass from runner to runner in Tito's relay race (the symbol of brotherhood and unity) has returned as the fratricidal truncheon, the gun, the knife with which male representatives of the former Yugo-peoples are annihilating each other. The towns and villages traversed in the past by the relay race are being toppled today like houses of cards in almost the identical order, from north to south. The collective human body has turned into a mass of human flesh, all ex-Yugoslavs today are mere man-meat. The fact that some perish as Croats, others as Serbs, others as Bosnians, as well as the fact that Bosnians are dying in the largest numbers, is not a matter of consequence for death.

In this utterly deranged, broken world, strains of the former and present regimes intermingle, melodies we've know from before but are now hearing in a new arrangement, symbols we've seen before but are seeing in a new design. In this new reality, a surrealistic nightmare, kitsch has shown the greatest tenacity, it was the quickest to adapt and come to life again in all its irrepressible splendor. In this country that has cracked to pieces, its kitsch has also fractured: each side has salvaged shards from the ruins and glued them together as new strategic monsters.

The Croatian, Catholic, folklore version of kitsch has reinvented itself by manufacturing a composite of ancient stone monuments and Celtic knotwork, Catholic saints and crosses, gingerbread hearts, and folk costumes. Out of the ruins of what was once our shared home it has snatched Tito, who has suddenly risen from the dead in the person of the new Croatian president. He wears white jackets like Tito's; he gives children apricots from his garden (Tito sent Yugoslav children baskets of mandarins from his gardens); kisses, swings into the air, and pinches the cheeks of any child who happens to appear before him (all presidents kiss children). In the redesigned state extravaganzas, the new president has taken a more active role than Tito did. While Tito used to sit calmly, letting the people parade their skills before him, the new president joins right in. At the ceremony marking the day of Croatian independence, surrounded by young girls in Croatian folk costume, the president took part in a pantomime by tenderly placing a gold coin in an empty peasant's cradle (the symbol of the newborn state). For prosperity, wealth, and happiness.

Meanwhile, the other, Serbian, side has manufactured its own monster out of elements of hysterical Orthodoxy, mixing Orthodox icons with peasant footwear, a folklore yelp with Chetnik daggers and bearded cutthroats. Historical eras are being mixed as well: epic songs with the phantoms of unrecognized kings, and these with red communist stars, traditional guslas with bugles, bugles with gun barrels. The Serbian side has salvaged the gray suit of communism from the ruins of what was once our shared home and draped it over their president. In this nightmare of the elements where crimes are being committed in the name of God, people are being butchered in the name of anti-fascism, concentration camps are springing up in the name of protection from genocide—the Serbian president is turning into a monstrous icon.

But though the kitsch of today overlays the previous version like a double exposure, the two images are nevertheless distinct. Socialist kitsch proclaimed its ideology as brotherhood and unity, internationalism, social equality, and technological progress. Nationalist kitsch proclaims its fundamental ideas as national sovereignty and privilege for the individual based on the blood group with the rubber stamp, on ethnicity, on "blood and soil." Socialist kitsch had a future-oriented projection and therefore a strong Utopian bent. Nationalist kitsch draws its substance from a passionate submersion in "the essence of the ethnic being" and as such is past-facing and therefore without the Utopian bent. The key symbols for socialist kitsch were linked to labor and progress (hence, in their iconography, all those railways, trains, mines, highways, factories, and the sculptures of embracing peasants and workers). Meanwhile the key symbols of nationalist kitsch are linked to national identity (hence, in their iconography, all the coats of arms, knights, Catholic and Orthodox crosses, sculptures of historical heroes). And both kinds of kitsch employ an identical strategy of seduction.

There is, of course, another fundamental distinction. Socialist kitsch was created in peacetime, in a country that had a future. This newer kitsch is being smeared like cake icing over the appalling reality of war. In the nightmare of war, nationalist kitsch penetrates all the pores of daily life like a virus, transforming genuine horror into the horror of *poshlost*. The doleful drone of reporters, long drawn-out TV shots, images of dead bodies, burials, corpses wrapped in national flags, the ritual acceptance of military honors so like the taking of communion, horrors accompanied by newly composed Balkan caterwauling, hit songs threatening to annihilate the enemy with the gusto of folklore, the kitsch-driven propaganda industry of war—all of this is bubbling in a Balkan cauldron between tragedy and farce, suffering and indifference, compassion and cynicism, horror and parody.

The new kitsch is pointedly reminiscent of Gogol's swimmer in the lake, hugging the two swans and seducing the girl on the balcony. We have to add a few more details to Gogol's picture: the floating corpses, the drowned, the torched homes, the dead children, the shards . . . The essence of the choreography with the swans remains the same: seduction. Our swimmers—the elected and self-appointed Balkan powermongers and their followers—seduce both Europe, who is knitting away up there on the balcony, and their own peoples, who are crouched, starving and impoverished, on the shore. The large, scowling, perspiring heads of our Balkan swimmers amid the waves ignore the unbefitting stage. And, as always, seduction wins. The peoples on the shore, each on their own side, applaud ecstatically; they see the performance as "the essence of their national being," as something beautiful, grand, and true. Defeat they perceive as triumph. "For in the kingdom of *poshlost*," as Nabokov says, thinking of literature, "it is not the book that 'makes a triumph' but the 'reading public' . . ."

"Do you think kitsch is a typical product of the communist system?" asked an American student after a lecture about Milan Kundera's novel *The Unbearable Lightness of Being.*

My student's innocent question precisely captures the seductive nature of kitsch. We are rarely aware of our own kitsch. It surrounds us, we breathe it in like air, it lives with us as our daily life, it shifts from the ugly to the beautiful, from the grotesque it becomes the aesthetic norm.

I don't know much about American kitsch. I don't know all its facets. I only know that in America, kitsch or garbage or trash is the most tasteful. I sometimes imagine America as a gigantic vacuum cleaner sucking in everything it comes across and throwing out alluring bales of trash. Trash is elevated here to the rank of a cosmic principle:

garbage is produced in order to be consumed, garbage is thrown out in order to be produced anew. Trash is everywhere, trash is the genetic cipher of the human species, as America has most clearly recognized. Its strength is in its indestructibility, its elasticity, its potential for transformation and mimicry, its recyclability. The strength of garbage lies in our need for it. It is inside us, as indestructible as fatty cells. You can slim down as you like, but the fatty cells are always there, lying in wait for their moment to be revitalized. Trash is expansive, trash has the tenacious character and the habits of the desert. In ecology the process is known as desertification. In cultural ecology the process is called trashization.

Paul Fussell, one of the most lucid of contemporary American "cultural ecologists," favors a new, broader definition of trash, as BAD. The meaning of Fussell's BAD is quite distinct from that of the word "bad." So, what is BAD? "It is something phony, clumsy, witless, untalented, vacant, or boring that many Americans can be persuaded is genuine, graceful, bright, or fascinating." Besides, to identify *BAD*, to be constantly on one's guard, offers one the satisfaction of feeling one is living in an age that "is teeming with raucously overvalued emptiness and trash." Fussell will say that a thing that is obviously bad will not remain bad for long, because someone will dream up something and *bad* will become *BAD*, it will be praised everywhere as valuable, desirable.

Despite all the efforts of anthropologists, cultural ecologists like Paul Fussell, "media ecologists" like James B. Twitchell, various experts on "garbage-ology," garbage, kitsch, junk, trash, and BAD are all aspects of the same unstoppable process. In this disintegrating, fragmented postmodern time—when all borders and hierarchies are being erased, when rights for everyone and for everyone the right to everything are being accorded through its universal mirror structure, at a time of personalization, at a time when the borders between high and low, art and non-art, are fading, a time of indifferent consumer bulimia, a time of atrophied senses—all doors are wide open to garbage, garbage permeates all the pores of life.

One evening, driving home from a concert, my friend Norman and I were dumbfounded by what surfaced from a dark underpass and knocked against the windshield like a sudden nightmare. In the darkness of the underpass was a heap of plush pandas waiting to be trucked somewhere. Pandas of all sizes, flung onto a heap like corpses, the faces expressing good-natured black-and-white death; this plush kitsch that showed its face in the dark underpass, looked to us like a sort of resumé, a hologram glint of our global future.

Trash in America is the most tasteful. If I had to choose among kitsch, *poshlost*, and trash, between *bad* and *BAD,* I would choose straightforward, unpretentious trash. Trash, garbage that does not conceal its nature, which is unambiguous, vulgar. When I feel like some of that trash, I buy popcorn and the *Weekly World News*, my favorite American paper, stretch out in an armchair and read. I toss popcorn rhythmically into my mouth and devour my reading matter: I learn that Elvis Presley is alive, parish priest Sam Beatty has testified to this; I learn that Gary Cormieru has built a submarine in his garage, that Claude Marquezy, a bank robber killed several years ago, now a ghost, is still on the rampage, leaving his fingerprints for the hapless policemen, I learn about dead pets that come back to haunt their homes, I inform myself about the Russian murderer who has butchered a hundred women and children, about animals that react to UFO signals, that JFK is alive, that the thinnest woman in the world has just become pregnant, that a man frozen in 1936 has come to life; I can learn how to contact my guardian angel, and that next year extra-terrestrial beings are going to attack the Earth, or so the astronomer Martin Stack assures me, I can read about the greatest surgeon in the world, Dr. Enrique de Pareda who is blind, about Gary Kosowsky, a teacher who killed his colleagues at school with Christmas candies dipped in poison, I can be taught how to telephone grave to grave, learn all there is to know about the chair of death that has killed 63 people since 1702, about Wes Haskins who eats three packs of cigarettes a day, about the dead bodies of Chinese astronauts that are orbiting the Earth, about all the evidence confirming that there is life after death, about human salamanders, about Ruth Lawrence who grows a little fatter by the second, about the fact that a moonquake in a few days' time will break the moon in two, about the famous hermaphrodite Anna Malreaux who impregnated herself and is now expecting a baby, I can read the authentic confession of a cannibal for whom children are his favorite item on the menu because they taste like fish. And when all this begins to bore me I can, according to the instructions of Swami Sudhanami Bundara in the same newspaper, simply fly away. I need only to be relaxed, visualize myself flying, hold my breath, concentrate on my movements, visualize my destination, and endeavor to stay as long as possible in the air.

American television produces a lifestyle, it forms taste, emotions, introduces new topics into circulation. In the flood of the new American touchy-feely, undisguised sentimentality, the new, "better quality" attitude to life, I clearly note the way the television model is reflected in everyday life and becomes kitsch. In Middletown there is a shop run by Italians. The owner's name is Romeo. And everything is as it ought to be, everything is in real life the way it is in the TV series about a friendly, appealing neighborhood where ethnicities mingle. And as I wait in line for my mozzarella I can't tell whether this is the life that gave rise to the television series or the television series gave rise to this life. Everything, as I say, is as it should be. The Italian is a sharp-tongued, scowling griper, gruff in his replies. The customers ahead of me inquire in cooing tones: What's the salad today, Romeo, should basil be added to the mozzarella, if so, then tell me, Romeo, is this one here fresh, and what about these olives, Romeo, and these artichokes, and how are the kids, Romeo . . . And while I stand in line, teeth clenched—I, the grumpy East European for whom conversations in line are deeply distasteful—a scene plays out between shopkeeper and customer before my eyes. I experience the scene like a one-act play, a dramatized guidebook on good-neighborly relations, on chit-chat, a manual about how to carry on a short, warm conversation, how to establish old-fashioned amicable relations with "your butcher," "your grocer." I see unfolding before my eyes an exercise in something long since lost, a sort of imitation of museum emotions, an attempt at establishing something that was never ours, nostalgia an act, kitsch. And, if I alter my perspective for a moment, what yawns from my example is a devastating solitude: both the customer's and mine, the observer's. And I'm immediately struck by the thought: is not kitsch itself a summons to overcome solitude, a summons to warm community.

"The new Goddess of Dullness is in the saddle, attended by her outriders Greed, Ignorance, and Publicity. In short, BAD has gotten such a head start that nothing can slow it down much, even if we should blow up the teachers' colleges; nationalize the airlines; make C, not B, the average grade again; reinstall Latin in the high schools; stop demeaning the children by calling them kids and policemen by calling them cops; get rid of intercollegiate athletics; curb the national impulse to brag; raise the capital gains tax; teach a generation to sneer at advertising and to treat astrology with contempt; build bridges that don't collapse; stay out of space; persuade educated people that criticism is their main business; speak and write English and other languages with some taste and subtlety; get the homeless into a new Civilian Conservation Corps; produce intelligent movies; develop in the Navy higher standards of courage and discipline; start a few sophisticated national newspapers; give diners at BAD restaurants the guts to say, after the manager has asked them if they've enjoyed their dinner, 'No'; abandon all remains of the self-congratulatory Cold War psychosis; improve the literacy of public signs and the taste of public sculpture; get people of artistic talent to design our stamps and coins; and develop public television into a medium free of all commerce. Because these things are not likely to happen, the only recourse is to laugh at BAD. If you don't, you're going to have to cry."

Unlike Fussell, I think there is hope. What fills me with confidence in American trash is that it always costs something. Because I'm afraid of free trash. That's the worst: we don't choose it, it chooses us.

Report

"On May 20 1992, at West 81 & 82nd Street & Bway about 23:00 in Teacher's Cafe a woman's purse was stolen. In it were $200, an address book, a checkbook, a bank card, keys, ID, social security card."

This complaint report was compiled by a tired black woman at a deserted precinct illuminated by a dim, greasy light. The name of the woman who typed the report indifferently, the last for that evening, was Jones ("complaint report prepared by Jones"). The person whose purse had been stolen was me. The reconstruction of the events in Jones's report looked like this:
"At t/p/o, complt. states above did approach her table asking for money Complt. states she gave her a token and her bag was next to her feet on the floor. Perp. picked up her bag and fled. Complt. able to identify perp."

So what is an event? One person stole another person's purse. If that's an event, is Police Officer Jones's report a real description of the everyday theft of a purse?

I try to compile my own report. After all, it was my purse that was stolen.

Norman, Madeline, and I were wandering around the Upper West Side, looking for a restaurant. It was Norman's birthday.
"It's Goran's birthday, too," I said.
"Who's Goran?" asked Norman.
And while I was explaining who Goran is, Madeline stopped us in our tracks and suggested we go to Teacher's Cafe. We sat down outside, a low barrier dividing us from the passersby. We talked about all sorts of things, and because it was Norman's birthday we talked about how life begins at forty.

"I remember I was about fifteen when I read that sentence somewhere. At the time it filled me with dread. Today I'm not feeling anything," said Norman.

An elderly bag lady walked past and examined our plates.
"Oh, broccoli!" she said, benevolently eyeing my plate. "Broccoli is not for me. George and I can't stand it," she said brightly and walked on.
"Who's George?" I asked.
"Bush," said Norman.

For some reason I felt I had to tell them about how I'd purchased tokens that day in the subway at Astor Place station. A Jamaican with an irresistible smile had been standing next to the booth where I bought them. I gave him the change. But some time later on in the subway, I decided not to give money to an armless cripple.
"No one was giving him money," I said.
"Such is life, always unfair," said Madeline.
"It's usually blacks who give money to cripples here," observed Norman.

Then there she was, a black woman. She circled around like a cat, muttering something incomprehensible, her hand outstretched. I fingered the tokens in my pocket, the ones I'd bought at Astor Place that morning.
"I have only tokens," I said.
"Okay," she said.
I handed her the little pieces of metal, she snatched them and vanished at once.

A few minutes later I noticed my purse was missing. We stood up. I tried, aloud, to recall the contents. Address book, keys to Goran's apartment, and keys I'd been given just a few hours before to the apartment of American friends who'd gone to Canada for a few days. There was money in the purse which I'd borrowed that morning from Goran. I had just one token left in my pocket.

When he discovered what had happened, the owner of the restaurant didn't charge us. Norman was agreeably surprised. For a moment we all forgot about the purse. Norman shook our host by the hand.
"Thank you," he said.
"That's what we do when this happens," said our host graciously.
We went to the nearest precinct to report the theft. The report was compiled by a tired black woman named Jones.

Then we went to the apartment of my friends, the ones who'd gone to Canada for a few days, and rang the super's bell. It took him a long time to respond.
"The super is sure to be a Yugoslav, all supers in New York today are Yugoslavs," said Madeline.
"Serbs, Croats, Albanians," Norman corrected her. At last the super appeared. We explained what had happened.
"I can't give you the key, but I'll let you in," said the grumpy Pole.

So what is an event? One person stole another person's purse. And is my report a true description of the everyday theft of a purse?

Today, May 21st, I am sitting shut up in my friends' New York apartment. I don't have a key, I'm afraid to go out. I peer into the windows of the neighboring buildings, I open the refrigerator, I nibble the remains of other people's food, feeling all the while the tepid gaiety of a mouse, I wrap myself in a blanket, snuggle into someone else's bed. I'm afraid that if I go out, if I stir, if I do anything, I'll pull out another thread, I'll unravel the last remaining shred of reality. Because I'm in someone else's apartment, the key to which I've lost, I'm in a strange city with no ID and no money, which was borrowed money anyway. Everything had been spirited away into the warm New York night by a feral black cat.

As I mull over the previous day I shake out every detail, as if dumping them from my purse. I assemble a puzzle in my mind, arranging the little pieces of the day, each one a symbol of loss. And it's as though each piece complements and explains the next. I read the previous day the way a fortune-teller reads a palm. I reflect on how all things mean more than they do and how the police language of Police Officer Jones is the only way to describe the event. Her language confirms that reality exists. All other language annuls it. And in my thoughts yet again I rewrite my report.

Goran's apartment is like a shoebox. He keeps a cot under his bed for guests passing through. For the time being I am his only guest. In the morning, while Goran gets ready to go to work, I stay in bed, any movement would further reduce what is in any case a very small space. Still half-asleep, I tell Goran my dream.

I'd dreamed about a cat, the color of a peach, dressed in a pink, silk waistcoat. "Help me take off my waistcoat, I can't walk in it," said the cat. "All right," I said.

It'll get dirty anyway, I thought as I held the touching little scrap of silk. Sad, I watched the cat and its paw prints in the dust for a long time as it walked away,

"I'd like to be like that cat," I told Goran from the bed.

"Describe it," said Goran.

"I can't," I said, "in dreams things are wonderful or terrible but not describable."

"Perhaps you're right. I often laugh in my sleep," said Goran, "but I never know why."

I lie in bed dozing for a long time after Goran goes to work. I summon dreams, prolong them, tug at them, stretch them out, swallow them with difficulty like the dry stuff of cotton candy. I feel sweat running down my neck. The din of New York soaks into the windows, the walls. New York is clamped in a vice of the three "H"s: Hot—Humid—Hazy. I ought to get up, I ought to come up with something for the day, I have to pick up the keys at five, I have to buy a bag, throw a few things into the bag. I mustn't let the three "H"s melt my resolve, transform me into narcoleptic dough, rock me in a tropical doze . . .

At noon I'm walking along 14th Street. The street dazzles, and the intensity of the glare makes my eyes sting. Human flesh rolls toward me: faces with a greasy sheen, a broad bottom in the grip of a cheap polyester skirt, bleached hair with dark roots, fat arms, sweat stains on a shirt. As if caught in an invisible meat grinder, I'm sucked into the funnel of the sweaty, greasy crush of humanity, the human race vending hot dogs on the street corners, combing the market for cheap merchandise, seeking a little something for themselves, the human race trundling things in and trundling them out, buying and selling cheap booty: their rags, their outmoded clothes, the shiny silver sandals surfacing from who knows what corner of the world, neckties, bedding, carpets, household goods, food . . . Teeming humanity with a hankering for leather, leather jackets, bags, belts. The women wear shoes, crooked high heels, and little chains on their ankles that glint through their cheap nylon stockings; the men with their narrow derrieres, and gold chains slung around their necks. This slice of humanity favors flashy rings; gold chains, gold bracelets gleam everywhere, and they buy and sell audio and video systems: VCRs, loudspeakers, radios. All over the world, vendors like them peddle watches, they infiltrate everywhere with their watches, as if they themselves are the cult object. They are of a kind who, even when camouflaged, even when inhabiting a different social orbit, betray themselves as—drawn irresistibly by a secret signal—they stop at stands run by others like them. These are the peddlers who at the Zagreb market repeat in a nasal drone: "watches, watches, watches," they sling cheap drugs on Washington Square with the same drone, the same cadence, the same furtive look. As a race they are preserving from oblivion a relic of their world, they are a museum race playing saws, barrel organs and Jew's harps, dancing the Argentinian tango in the New York subway. A race selling little talismans; knives, openers, potato dicers, magical potions for removing all kinds of stains. A race that bamboozles, selling hair scrunchies, balloons, plush monkeys playing cymbals, plastic frogs floating in dirty pools, tin chickens pecking at the pavement. A race that always, everywhere in the world, sells and buys bags: big émigré suitcases that stand chained together out in front of the store and have room inside for a person's entire life, bags of all shapes and sizes; a race that seems to have nothing better to do than buy these bags and suitcases, that seems to think about nothing but buying a suitcase and setting off for an unknown destination, only to surface someplace else. A race that tells fortunes on the street, reads palms or cards, spins a crystal ball and reads this world's fortune, a race that juggles balls everywhere on earth, does conjuring tricks, engages in sleight of hand and petty fraud, a race that begs, a race that gives off its yelps, mixing languages, drenching my ear with sounds like hot wax. A race that is dirty, warm, toothless, that feeds New York, nourishing it with blood, filling its capillaries, a race that is gesturing clearly to difference, a race that despises its clean, tidy, white, fresh, icy, chilled, its aseptic, other face.

It's noon, I'm walking along 14th Street, the one to which the hero of Jay McInerney's novel refuses to descend because he doesn't have the "lowlife" visa. I walk freely, I have the visa, these are my people, I sniff them out, I know what they are saying even when they're speaking Arabic, Russian, Spanish, Turkish, Greek, Polish. They live on Canal Street, on 14th Street, on the Lower East Side, on Orchard, Delancey, on the Bowery, in Chinatown, in Harlem, on the edges of Manhattan, between C and D Avenues, they emerge everywhere like moles on immaculate lawns, they circulate through the underground yellow, red, green, blue veins of the city.

I'm walking at noon along 14th Street, I buy cashew nuts from a street vendor, I eat them greedily, as if I'm starving, enveloped by my sweaty, greasy, warm race. I go into stores, the thought that I need to buy a bag pulsing rhythmically in my befuddled brain, I talk to the vendors, they make offers, knock the price down, sputter in anger. I stop beside the bamboozlers, the ones who in the smallest possible space, on little folding stools, on a low concrete wall, on the bare pavement, set out their miniature magician's props: a little ball and cup. I follow the ball, the swift, sponge mouse, here it is, I say, he lifts the cup, the ball is lying there calmly like a promise, you guessed right, he says, here's your prize, let's have another go. He wraps me in words like cotton candy, the little ball rolls, flees, vanishes, reappears, the crowd sighs, makes its sounds, communal sweat runs down our backs.

I didn't buy a bag.
Instead of a bag I bought the nuts.
I ate the nuts.
I roamed the streets, dazed by the heat.
I gave money to the Jamaican with the irresistible smile.
"Good luck," said the Jamaican for some reason.
I went back to Goran's apartment.
I took my toothbrush and nightgown. I got into a taxi.
"You have a headache," said the driver.
"No. Why?"
"You keep rubbing your temples," he said.
In the mirror I see his gray-green eyes.
A bandanna tied over his forehead, an irresistible smile.
I'm suddenly overcome by the tired thought that I'm growing old.
I get out of the taxi.
"Good luck," says the white Jamaican for some reason.
"Good luck," I say and because of a momentary rush of furtive shame, I give him a larger tip than I should have.

Shut up in someone else's apartment, I compose my report, I run through the episodes of the previous day like a movie script, I work out the timing, attend to the rhythm, calculate, repeat. Two birthdays, two irresistible smiles, two bags, one unbought and one stolen. And I don't succeed in pulling the story together into a logical report. But it does make me think that everything in this world is connected. Even the most distant worlds are connected by secret threads. The sweaty slice of humanity on 14th Street spins swift little balls, covering them with little cups, sweaty humanity purrs, draws the gazes of passersby to the little balls, enchants, cheats, the wily sweaty magicians perform their cheap skill, not knowing it is perhaps worlds they're spinning.

I stare into the New York night, thinking that the theft was the legitimate end of yesterday's story, an incomprehensible screenplay written in the hot New York day by the three "H"s. I think about my black sister. Maybe she's already using my name, maybe as of tomorrow I'll be begging for money on the New York streets, circling around tables like a cat. Or I'll do that in one of my dreams. Everything is everything. In a soft carnival New York night, black-cat shadows slink through town, scratching and purring, tying threads into little knots of destiny. In the soft New York night the stars clink like subway tokens, pass quietly from pocket to pocket, twinkling like the Jamaican's smile. Black is white, white is black, loss is gain, gain is loss. New York sparkles like a magical puzzle. I let the cat from my dream pad away without its silk waistcoat. Maybe, as in the old Chinese tale, it was the cat dreaming me. Somewhere along the border between sleep and waking there is struck a balance, somewhere the puzzle piece falls into place, somewhere all debts are paid.

That's what I'm thinking tonight. But tomorrow, to survive, I'll reduce reality to the comprehensible language of Police Officer Jones. Because everything else would, of course, be a fairy tale.

Coca-Cola

Recently, Coca-Cola opened a location on the fanciest stretch of Fifth Avenue, a nostalgia store stocking Coca-Cola merchandise. The store sells key rings, wastebaskets, umbrellas, T-shirts, ties, caps—everything of course bearing the Coca-Cola logo. You can buy replicas of Coca-Cola coolers with built-in radios, clocks, toys, dancing Coca-Cola cans sporting eyeglasses, badges, Frisbees, balls, commemorative Coca-Cola bottles delivered by antique Coca-Cola slot machines, cassettes with Coca-Cola tunes (the Coca-Cola rag, bush, waltz, polka). You can buy souvenir glasses, trays, plates, everything, of course, in the red-and-white Coca-Cola colors. There are Coca-Cola ads for sale in all the languages of the world, and posters and books: *The Mix Guide to Commemorative Coca-Cola Bottles*; *Coca-Cola—The First 100 Years*; *The Chronicle of Coca-Cola Since 1886*; *The Encyclopedia of Coca-Cola Collectibles*; *The Ladies of Coca-Cola*, and finally, books about the Coca-Cola Superstars. You can buy special cans of Coca-Cola produced by NASA for consumption in zero-gravity conditions. You can read the dying words of a certain J. P. Day who, on his deathbed, said: "I die in peace, knowing I'll find Coca-Cola in heaven!"

In a red booth, in the shape of a Coca-Cola can, there's an interactive computer. With the touch of a finger you can click on icons displaying topics from the hundred-year history of the product. The history of an ordinary drink that is 90 percent water and 10 percent sugar and, with a little caramel, caffeine, and CO_2 becomes a chronicle of money, business, industrial progress, ideology, the media, culture—a history of modern civilization. In the same year, 1886, America offered the world the Statue of Liberty and Coca-Cola; the grand idea and the grand pacifier.

And as I touch the screen and sip the cloying reddish-brown liquid, linking thereby into the mega-bloodstream of more than 350 million people in 155 countries, as I drink the sacred Nothing and align my pulse with the heartbeat of the millions, I suddenly seem to see on the screen, in a ghostly hologram, the flash of a knife.

"In a famous tale from the frozen north," says M. B., a Serbian poet whose poem I am paraphrasing here in prose, "wolf hunters dip their double-edged dagger in blood, plunge the hilt into the ice and leave it in the snowy wasteland. The hungry wolf picks up the scent of the blood from afar, especially in that clean, sharp air under the high frozen stars, and quickly finds the bloody bait. Licking the frozen blood it cuts its long tongue and soon it's lapping its own warm blood from the cold blade. It cannot stop until it drops to the ground, bloated with its own blood. If this is what wolves, so difficult to hunt, are like, then what chance do people, and whole peoples, have, especially ours, who cannot get enough of their own blood. They would sooner vanish than face the fact that the bloody dagger is all that remains as our sole monument and cross."

The lines by Serbian poet M. B. were published in 1989 in a Belgrade literary journal. The metaphor he used soon turned into reality. Once his words were uttered they were out there and the Great Evil was hatched from the serpent's egg. One day, when that reality reverts to metaphor, the symbols will remain behind like monuments and crosses hovering over the blotches of different colors on the map. The Coca-Cola here, the knife there. Squeezed between the two symbols—one leering in a sudden hologram and the other in the can I'm clutching—and paralyzed by the image on the screen, I stand and shudder. And caught in this coincidental flash of the two cultures—one that transforms nothing into *the real thing* and the other that transforms *real things* into nothing, one that appeals to life and the other that summons death, one that creates its history out of senselessness and the other that transforms its history into senselessness, one that erects a temple to an ordinary bottle and the other that grinds up its real temples like glass, one that appeals to the future and the other that recalls the past, one that waves its red-and-white colors and the other that shrouds everything in black, one that seeks international brotherhood through sugar water and the other that demands a brotherhood in blood—I choose the first. The other leers out of the holographic depths with its own version of slogans: *Have a Knife and smile. Knife is it. When a Knife is part of your life, you can't beat the feeling. A Knife adds life. Things go better with a Knife—a Knife is the real thing. What you want is a Knife. A Knife is just right. A Knife . . . the pause that brings friends together. Wherever you go you'll find a Knife. Knife . . . after Knife . . . after Knife . . .*

Squeezed between these two symbols, between the two cultures, one transforming nothing into *the real thing* and the other transforming *real things* into nothing, I bow to the former. I drink the caramel emptiness, the sweet reddish liquid courses through my veins, nourishing the capillaries of the world. We are communicating vessels, we are the mega-bloodstream, us 350 million.

I leave the store and point my body toward Central Park. I feel a cloying nausea in my belly, I feel conciliation. The knife that appeared in the sudden flash of my brain is gone. I walk toward Central Park whispering . . . Blessed be thy name, oh holy bottle, Coca-Cola, thanks be unto John S. Pemberton who conceived thee, unto Asa G. Cander who bequeathed thee his faith and funds, unto Frank Robinson who gave thee a name, unto Joseph A. Biedenbarn who placed thee in a bottle . . . Blessed be thy name, oh holy emptiness, myth, simulation, blessed be thy name, oh Idea, oh Coca-Cola, oh Superstar . . . Who needs reality. I give my all for the bubbles!

Cappuccino

I'm afraid of velvet. Velvet is ambiguous, warm, and seductive. At night broken glass shimmers on the New York pavement like velvet. The homeless wrapped in their grimy tatters adorn themselves with the brilliance of the pavement and shimmer in the dark like mysterious messengers from outer space. At night the din is as mum as velvet. Sounds sleep behind heavy steel shutters. When the last shutters roll down in the evening, a sharp bang rends the air and then all is still again. The warm pavement absorbs sounds like velvet. If I find myself out on the street late at night, I walk with great care because the world in the darkness eludes my control. The city wraps around me like hot velvet and I am afraid I'll stay forever, growing into the pavement, melting into it. I'm afraid of velvet, as I said. Because velvet is as ambiguous, warm, and seductive as madness.

That is why I like morning. The shapes are firm, the sounds clear, the city comes alive in its verticals and horizontals, sharp, bright, and unambiguous. Like a compass needle, the morning drives away the velvet shadows of the night. In the morning, the world is again under my control. The little square in my organizer determines my morning route: 11:00 A.M., a meeting with Sally.

Installed at Borgia Café, gazing at the fresh bread in the little, bright green window of Vesuvio Bakery, I order my first cappuccino of the morning. I sit, blow off the thick foam sprinkled with rust-colored cinnamon and supervise the life of the street. The inhabitants of the street stroll lazily along. Dressed hastily in whatever they could grab, they go down to the first store to pick up breakfast and the morning papers or take their dog for a walk. The morning sun slides lazily over the façades of the buildings. Objects gleam in the shop windows: in one, a golden horse's head, in another, fresh grass, in a third, trees painted silver, in a fourth, a wooden angel with baseball cap on head. A young man passes by carrying a cello, another sips from a can as he walks, down the street come cyclists, tourists. Workers emerge from somewhere hauling packages in and out. They all swap and shuffle like cards in the hands of invisible card-players.

I drink my cappuccino and supervise the life of the street. Trucks pass by; the names written on their sides form a moving alphabet: C—for Casalino, R—for Riteway Laundry, M—for Milady's, W—for Wellcraft. Colors prance: strident green, strident red, pink, sea-blue, the green-and-white arrows and red octagons of stop signs. In the Chinese laundries on thin wire hangers chime suits in transparent plastic bags, fire-escapes wind around buildings like black metal vines, antennas and water tanks jut, trucks and cars chug, bottles rattle, fire truck sirens wail, the languages of the passersby pour into my ear.

I drink my cappuccino and supervise the life of the street, I retrace its route in my mind, feel its pulse, check the balance, subject myself to a mental *walk-don't walk* rhythm. Homeless people on Washington

Square sleep curled up on benches, mothers take their children to the playground; children, drug dealers, students, drunks, builders, chess-players, all buzz in a groggy morning reconciliation . . . Don't walk. The large, blonde owner of Pandora's Box, surrounded by statues of plaster angels, picks up her phone in the shape of a woman's pink shoe. Walk. Young men play basketball on the court, idle onlookers consume their morning snack out of brown paper bags. Don't walk. Black kids wipe the windshields of cars at the corner. My nostrils breathe in the pungent aroma of marijuana. A young man on the corner inhales his last puff and, throwing away the stub, disappears. Walk. Greasy oil paint melts in the sun, peeling thickly off the rib-like railings. Clouds float lazily across the sky. On top of a building, workers are writing "Girls Love Boys" with a paintbrush. The brush caresses the letter L. Don't walk . . . Mentally I take the pulse of the city, I feel the pavement slowly warming, soon a pavement haze will rise, and with it everything becomes possible.

I look at my watch. The hands point to 11:20 a.m. The pavement around me slowly vaporizes heat. I calmly blow the thick foam sprinkled with rust-colored cinnamon from my second or third cappuccino, light a cigarette, and, there, Sally's coming. We exchange kisses, she sits. With her full lips, with two little lines sloping sadly downward, Sally forms her words properly, like soap bubbles. Her children have grown and moved away, her husband left her, and at one moment everything slipped out of her control, she stopped smoking, that helped a bit, and then John, her best friend, gay, a writer like herself, developed AIDS, and then the Mexicans came . . . What Mexicans? Cleaners at the college, first one family, then they brought their brothers and sisters along, fourteen of them, now there are fourteen, they clean the college, they clean up our shit, says Sally. They were so helpless, they didn't know a word of English, nor their rights. She took it all upon herself, all for free, she's teaching them English, now they've wrapped around her, they bought her a Thanksgiving turkey, why do foreigners think turkey is an American cult worth following, she personally can't bear the institution of the Thanksgiving turkey, especially since her life went to pieces, the children grew up, and everything has slipped from her control. In a word, they've latched onto her, she is the compass in their émigré darkness, they keep coming, they come when they're in trouble, they come when she's in trouble, there's something warm in the Mexican crowd, but the turkey really touched her, especially when she thought about how they had no money, poor things, now her house was full, her life had gone to pieces, there was no order any more, no tranquility, no sleep, everything had definitively slipped from her control. The Mexicans often cried, sang, laughed, a strange people those Mexicans, they cried with her when John died, though they'd never met him, John was a God-given talent, oh God, how many people are dying of AIDS here, if you only knew, all of it with John was so dreadful, hard for her to bear, the loss . . .

I see the two sad little lines on Sally's face puckering her mouth like invisible pins, she's going to cry.

"How's your novel going?" I ask.

Ah, a strange thing happened, actually everything began when John died. Something snapped, she woke up one night and half-asleep, in her nightgown, she sat down at the computer, she didn't budge for the next three days and nights and wrote the first hundred or so pages in Spanish, so that's how it started, and she realized she wasn't lost after all, that she'd bring her life back into control, that she'd write her novel.

"You know Spanish?" I ask, impressed.

"No. Why do you ask?" says Sally.

And in the gleam of her eye I catch sight of that dark, seductive, velvety sheen.

"I just thought . . ." I say.

A chance glimpse of my watch shows it is 2:35 p.m. The little table of Borgia Café, the two cups of cappuccino, and the two of us, Sally and I, are slowly vanishing in the dense, golden, pavement haze.

Bagel

If I had to choose between a doughnut, a muffin, and a bagel, I'd always go for the bagel without a moment's hesitation. Although I admit there's something to be said for the doughnut.

A doughnut is a small, ring-shaped, deep-fried bun, as Webster's Dictionary says. A doughnut is a cheap, simple, common American pastry. Variants on this simple fried dough, devoid of imagination, this dumpling with a hole, this amicable round bun, have taken over diners, American supermarket freezers, and fast-food stands. I admit there's something alluring to its plump good-naturedness, its wholesome color, in its simple pastry heart. To taste the real thing, go to a rural bakery. There you'll see armies of swelling, golden-brown doughnuts boldly emerging. The essence of the doughnut is not only its simple nature but also its sociability. A doughnut simply cannot be experienced in the singular, because it hardly exists in the singular. A doughnut is always doughnuts. When doughnuts bought at a farm stand are put into a paper bag, the heady aroma of the cinnamon makes the customer giddy. At the same time, the bag must not be closed. The doughnut, whose charm is in any case of brief duration, lives on air. Lack of oxygen will transform it into an indifferent lump of barely digestible dough, devoid of all appeal.

What can I say about the muffin? Webster tells us it is a small, domed, quick bread made from eggs and flour, baked in a mold and usually eaten while hot. I would say that the verbal satisfaction—coming from pressing together the upper and lower lips to make the sound "m" and then the slow rub of the upper teeth against the lower lip to make the sound of the double "ff"—is all the muffin has to offer. A muffin is a infantile form of mush, a hodge-podge, the muffin is a treat for the poor and the amateur, the muffin is not just simple, it's crude. It is a *nothing* simply by virtue of being an *anything*. The muffin has neither character nor consistency. The muffin shows a tendency to crumble. Besides, the quality of any food can be measured by a simple test: can it be eaten on its own? Ask yourself that question in the case of the muffin and you'll immediately feel your mouth go dry. The muffin cries out for us to wash it down with tea or milk. The muffin has no personality, the muffin is the zombie of breads.

As I said at the outset, when choosing among doughnuts, muffins, and bagels, I definitively go for the bagel. A bagel isn't a treat, it's a thing and it's food. In the case of bagels I do not agree with Webster, which describes it as a small (it isn't small at all!) bread roll (roll!) in the shape of a doughnut! *Doughnut-shaped*, that's what Webster says, which of course implies that the doughnut is older than the bagel, and that is a damned lie! Not only do bagels have their own long (Jewish) tradition, but they have stylistic subvariants in many countries, especially Slavic. This cosmopolitan form of baked good is known as the *bublica* in Dalmatia, the *bublik* in Russia, the *devrek* in Macedonia and Bulgaria. And that's just the Slavic countries.

A bagel is above all a ritual. On Sunday you have to pop down to the little Jewish bakery and buy a decent quantity of bagels. (A decent quantity, I say. Bagels also do not tolerate solitude!) Then you have to cut them in half, spread them with butter, and on top of the butter, like flower petals, scatter thin orange flakes of salmon. This is the classical, simple, elegant version. Tuna spread is good as well, and so is the laborer's salt-of-the-earth version with fresh herring and little rings of onion. Such a morning bagel is unimaginable without the Sunday edition of the *New York Times*. The fat Sunday edition must be spread over the table, place the bagels on the newspaper (the smell of the bread and printer's ink is important), make plenty of crumbs as you eat, leave greasy finger prints, and let the interplay of the food and printed text determine the path the reader's eye follows.

The strength of the bagel lies in its consistency, its tangibility. Only a fool would hold a muffin in his hand, while a greasy, knobbly doughnut is a tactile insult. A bagel with its smooth, taut crust, its firm round body, fits perfectly into the curve of the palm. The bagel sits in the hand as if molded to it, in its natural bed it is a divine disc. The bagel plays naturally with the hand, it fits naturally like a ring on a finger: the finger likes it and the bagel feels good too. The larger, drier Slavo-Turkish version—the *devrek*—can be worn on the arm like a bracelet.

The essence of the bagel lies in the hole. The essence of the hole is visual. On Sundays, grab hold of a bagel and walk to Central Park, stop by the place where the roller skaters dance and bring the bagel to your eye . . . I look at the scene through the little hole. If it's too small, I hollow out the dough, enlarge the view. There's nothing odd about it, I'm peering through a bagel, so what. No one gets excited and why should they. It's a question of optics, I say. The detail, not the whole. The whole is too big, optically indigestible, it doesn't fit in the eye, doesn't reach the brain. A detail glides easily to the eye through the tunnel of ruddy dough. In time to the music a black tattooed forearm glides through the air, a muscle firm as an apple glides through the air, eyeglasses in a black-and-white frame glide by, a broad grin glides by, skates glide, a leg glides, a gold earring glides, looks glide . . .

Nestled in my little circle, like a mouse in a cheese, I survey the world. No one can do anything to me. And when I get bored, I take the dough ring off my eye, alter the optics, fold myself up like a telescope. I wander through Central Park, nibbling my bagel: half for me, half for the birds.

There, that's why I'll always vote for the bagel! That's why I'll always prefer bagels to muffins and doughnuts. Long live the bagel! Death to that blunder of egg and dough, the worthless muffin! As for the doughnut? Let it be.

Dreamers

You'll see us everywhere: on benches in parks, lying on the grass, our heads thrown back and mouths open, pressed up against the walls of houses, our arms folded under piles of rags, and you'll wonder in alarm whether the rags conceal a human frame or just its ghostly imprint, you'll see us everywhere. Sometimes sleep is so irresistible that we lie down mid-road, we haven't time to choose a place, you step around us with undisguised contempt. You'll see us in winter sleeping with our arms around vents that send out sweet, hot steam. You'll see us in the street talking to ourselves, muttering into our chins, sleeping as we walk, our eyes wide open, intently spinning the stuff of dreams. There are thousands of us, we are human larvae, Aborigines, we are dreamers.

When New York is gripped in the vice of the three "H"s (Hot-Humid-Hazy), when oppressive sultriness makes the concrete crumble, when the pavement melts beneath your feet, when the lungs fight for a gasp of oxygen, when the sky is as motionless as a glass dome, when a heavy golden haze shimmers in the air, when the sweet smells of decay waft in from all around—that's when you dream best.

I lie in a bed set up in the loft. I don't know what time it is. I'm in a capsule, a solitary example of the human species in my own Noah's Ark. The sunny haze ignites the room like a spotlight: it dissolves the walls, the iron railings, the pictures, the books, the floor, the ceiling . . . I stare at the huge windows, at the one and only reliable signpost—the green sign with white arrow pointing to the right: Canal St. The loft shakes. Beneath me flows Hudson Street, where jackhammers have been juddering for days now. The jackhammers gouge out ditches, yellow backhoes excavate earth mixed with concrete, old pipes are being replaced by new ones. Orange figures spray orange signs, lines, set up orange fences and barriers. The iron joists vibrate from the jackhammers, police sirens, cars, greasy beads of sweat soak through the walls. The throbbing from below seems to make the wooden water tanks at the level of my eyes rise slowly up into the air.

I lie like this and I know that soon the dusty, deserted park on the other side of the street will rise up to my fifth-floor windows and hover like a becalmed ship waiting for wind. Soon the throbbing in the depths will send the nearby police station up into the air, soon police officers on horses will ride out of the police station and trot slowly through the air . . . And then I, too, will float away. Because I am a dreamer. I am an Aborigine.

In my sticky, damp sleep I creep along the underground blood vessels of the city, its blue, red, green, and yellow veins, I turn for a moment into a gray vein toward Queens, then into a brown vein toward Brooklyn, and then I slowly rise, stop, and look around. My gaze polishes the Chrysler Needle, with the sandpaper of my gaze I smooth the sharp corners of the World Trade Center. On the Hudson River I see motionless sailboats pinned to the gray-blue silk ribbon; they look like dead butterflies. I blow softly, set them moving and smile in my sleep. On the Brooklyn Bridge the bridge-painters have fallen asleep, I rock them a little with my breath, and the brushes in their hands begin diligently spreading paint.

When New York is gripped in the vice of the three "H"s (Hot-Humid-Hazy), when oppressive sultriness makes the concrete crumble, when the pavement melts beneath your feet, when the lungs fight for a gasp of oxygen, when the sky is as motionless as a glass dome, when a heavy golden haze shimmers in the air, when the sweet smells of decay waft in from all sides, I most like launching my dreams from Ellis Island. I go there and flow into the bloodstream of millions of dead dreamers, they gurgle inside me in all the languages of the world, I am a Jew, a Pole, a Swede, I am African, Russian, Italian, I am white, black, and yellow. I walk beside a wall lined with copper plaques and run my sweaty fingertips, as if reading Braille, over the thousands of names engraved in the copper, I hear their voices, I absorb their destinies like blotting paper—and I dream.

As I run my fingers over the Braille letters I watch Manhattan. My gaze polishes the sharp corners of the World Trade Center, I'm used to performing this as an involuntary action. I look around me carefully: Manhattan is as motionless as a becalmed ship. The hot haze transforms the city into a fantastic fossil.

New York is not a city of dreams, it is a city built by us, the dreamers. As we dream, we're pressed groundward, this is why our city has shot so far up into the sky. Manhattan is the stuff of our dreams. From here, from Ellis Island, I absorb the energy of long-vanished dreamers, those thousands upon thousands who spent decades building the city on the other shore. Manhattan. A city at eye's reach. It was built by those who gawk, thrilled, through the windows of the Great Hall, those who, pressing their foreheads against the cold tiled walls, gazed at the other shore, those who sat on the bulky bundles in which they'd brought their past lives and dreamed of a new one, those who had spent months crushed below decks and then, when they arrived and disembarked, were awestruck. Their breath gave rise to the city. Perhaps the Czech peasant woman Anna Kudrinova exhaled the Empire State Building as she gazed longingly across at the other shore from Ellis Island.

What holds my gaze longest is the glass dome of the Winter Garden, nestled among the skyscrapers of the Financial Center, the only curved shape among the verticals. The dome is like a gigantic larva. It too is the work of dreamers. Out of the transparent dome of the Winter Garden, as from a gigantic popcorn-machine, new dreams are hatching. New York is an oneiric perpetuum mobile.

"I am one of millions who do not fit in, who have no home, no family, no doctrine, no firm place to call my own, no known beginning or end, no 'sacred and primordial site.' I declare war on all icons and finalities, on all histories that would chain me with my own falseness, my own pitiful fears. I know only moments, and lifetimes that are moments, and forms that appear with infinite strength, then 'melt into air.' I am an architect, a constructor of worlds, a sensualist who worships the flesh, the melody, a silhouette against a darkening sky. I can't know your name. Nor can you know mine. Tomorrow, we begin together the construction of a city," as Aborigine, dreamer, architect Lebbeus Woods inscribed his manifesto in the blistering air.

And so, when you see us lying on benches in the parks, pressed up against the walls of houses, sheltering in cardboard boxes, on the streets, in the subway, when you see us muttering to ourselves as we walk, spinning the stuff of our dreams, don't wake us . . . It could happen that unwittingly you'd be pulling the wrong thread and unraveling everything: yourself, the streets, the city, its dazzling image shooting up into the sky, and that you pull down the very sky itself . . .

Amnesia

RECENTLY I'VE BECOME increasingly forgetful. Driven by a sudden thought, I jump up from my desk, go to the bookshelf, and then stop. My eyes roam over the titles, I simply cannot remember what it was I came for. Driven by a practical thought I stride briskly to the bathroom and stop. I simply cannot remember why I came. I look at myself in the mirror, stand like that, face to face with myself, a sudden dizziness comes over me, a stab of anxiety. I return, sit down in the armchair, bury my face in my hands. I rock my own face in my hands, think about nothing . . .

If I move my head slightly I can see the fire escape through the window, and on the steps—black leather boots. If I lean a little farther forward, I'll see a young man, my neighbor, someone I don't know. He sits on the steps every day. The tenant from the apartment above mine, he listens to music and, like a lazy cat, observes the life of the street, the corner of Beach and Hudson Streets, from the fire escape.

The young man on the steps has no idea that we're linked by a shared rhythm. He climbs out of his window, sits at his observation post, and watches the life of the street as if it were on a screen. Meanwhile, I switch on the television, nervously waiting for the news. Every half hour I see pictures of dismembered bodies at the Sarajevo open market. The same pictures.

Cocooned in my temporary New York shelter, in the half-hour intervals between the same pictures on the screen, I go over to the bookshelves, to the bathroom, bow my head, check to see whether the young man's boots are still there. For the thousandth time I ask myself questions for which I have no answer. I try to think, to remember, to reconstruct everything from the beginning, I try to find reasons. There is nothing in my head but throbbing pain. Plink-plonk. I try again, by a different, more cunning method: I collect the remains of the ruins in a little heap, I try to recollect my school, friends, journeys, cities, rivers, mountains, islands, just like that, from the beginning, starting with my first reading primer. Plink-plonk. Nothing but a dull pain throbs in my head. I try again, I try to remember the names of streets, the names of my friends in Sarajevo, in Dubrovnik, in Belgrade. In my memory appear houses with no numbers, streets with no name, names with no face or faces with no names, fragments, dissolving pictures, ripped-out sentences. Plink-plonk. The pain throbs. Everything lies in a gray zone of forgetting and doesn't move.

Viruses have invaded my memory. The snatch of a song pops into my head. *The native has a bow and arrow, railway line, village, town / may the country grow and thrive, long live, long live work.* A few lines from my early socialist reader—which ought, like one of the hundreds of thwarted keys still in my possession, to lead me to a new door, to the answers to the questions raised—but instead, suddenly, they are followed by the message *Frodo lives!*

The viruses invading my memory have cute names: *Best Wishes*, *Black Monday*, *Cascade*, *Chaos*, *Devil's Dance*, *Evil*, *Guppy*, *Joker*, *Perfume*, *Ping-Pong*. Viruses have invaded my memory. *Sorry. Not found.* At this very moment, there are viruses feeding on my country, human lives, history, monuments, viruses are feeding on the living, they are feeding on the dead. The masters of forgetting know their job. The gray zones of forgetting in my memory are completely legitimate: can I reconstruct my own history on a background that is no longer there? *Path not found. Sorry.* Down the screen of my memory slip pictures, fragments, sentences, words, they break into bits, into letters, the letters slide down like dead flies, they pool at the bottom, turning into a dark silt.

"So, gentlemen, you would like me to show you the house where I was born? But I came into the world in a hospital in Fiume and that hospital has been pulled down. You will not be able to put a plaque on the house where I lived, for it too has probably been pulled down. Or you could put up three or four plaques with my name on them in various towns and various countries, but I wouldn't be able to help there either, because I no longer remember where I lived as a child, I hardly know which language I spoke. What I remember are images: a palm waving and oleanders somewhere by the sea. The murky green Danube flowing past meadows, a counting rhyme: eenie-meeie-minie-mo . . ." as Danilo Kiš wrote.

Frodo lives, my virus consoles me. And off I go to my temple of amnesia, FAO Schwarz, the toy store on Fifth Avenue. I go up to the second floor and stop, hypnotized by the Swiss Jolly Ball, the grandest pinball machine in the world. Crammed in among international throngs of tourists, I gaze in wonder at the gadget by Charles Morgan. The crowd tensely follows the path of the little metal ball, holds its breath, sighs with relief, gasps with admiration. Switzerland has been squeezed into its symbols: on the model are a Swiss sun, a Swiss ski-lift, Swiss Alps, a blue Swiss train, Swiss cheese, a Swiss bus, Swiss bells, Swiss cows, Swiss chocolate, a Swiss bank . . . I watch the little metal ball sliding, rattling down the streets, mounting the peaks, rolling into the bank, the post office, the train, stopping—on its precise trajectory, mastering point after point on its terrain. Plink-plonk. The little ball shines with a holy metal gleam: the noisy god of forgetting is at his mechanical task.

The hypnotic journey of the little ball suits me, it soothes my inner nightmare by setting it to a regular rhythm. I enjoy the simplicity of the model, this is all I know about Switzerland and I don't seem to want to know more. I like the safe, mechanical journey of the ball. I follow its path with tense concentration, I wait for it to start again. I relish the painless, temporary amnesia, the simple, mechanical picture. One day my memory will be reduced to a like number of elements. No more, no less. The little ball of my memory will roll mechanically along its legitimate path. For a while, instead of real remembering, nothing but a dull pain will throb in my head. And then that, too, will pass. It will pass, too . . .

And now I think contentedly of returning to my apartment, climbing out the window, sitting down on the fire escape beside the young man I don't yet know in the leather boots and observing my corner, the corner of Beach and Hudson Streets.

I go outside. At the door I'm blinded by the sun. An old man, looking like a retired school teacher, is standing by the door with a rolled umbrella in hand.

"Is it raining?" he muses.

"I really wouldn't know," I reply.

Life Vest

From my starting point, the house on Hudson Street, I start unwinding like a skein of wool. God, I think in the taxi, will there be enough of me to last all the way to the airport? I stare through the trap of the taxi window, in a sudden surge of panic I try to retain images of New York in my memory, I wrap them around me as though I'm chilly. The images flash and disappear, unravel, stretch, sift through me like sand. With an effort of will I hold the last scene in the corner of my eye: the place caught by thousands of cameras, where the crosses in a cemetery in Queens merge for a moment with the verticals of Manhattan; they become a ship with the masts of Manhattan soaring above, its symbolic foundation, where for a moment Manhattan establishes its symbolic coordinates, its cross. That image is quickly supplanted by another, the last one, seen at John F. Kennedy Airport through the window of the plane just before takeoff. The little gray silhouettes on the horizon look like the buildings children make when they let soft sand pour through the funnel of their cupped fingers. The picture is so small that it fits into the eye. Manhattan is just the pale stroke of a paintbrush on the blue horizon. Scant gray mounds of indefinite outline: all that can be made out are the two tiny, elongated shadows of the World Trade Center and the little needle of the Empire State Building. Manhattan is a fragile medallion, a little watercolor held in the corner of my eye, to be washed away by the first tear.

The loudspeaker gurgles, giving first Dutch, then English. Our brief life in the air is determined by rituals and I follow them readily. I fasten my seat belt, unfasten my seat belt, follow the little lights as they come on and go off, smoke when the signals tell me I may, read the instructions with tense focus, reading the same text for the hundredth time, carefully follow the flight attendants' pantomime, respond in an orderly way to their plastic smiles, I take fruit juice, thank you, drink it down, thank you, gratefully accept the meal box, thank you, eat obediently, fiddle with the little packets of sugar, stroke them with my fingertips as though they are living beings, thank you, don my headphones, thank you, doff my headphones, thank you . . . Images of airport arrivals and departures run into one another in my head, overlapping. For some reason I remember my return from New York, three years earlier. It was a JAT plane, the company now gone because the country is gone, the comic wallpaper where your sleepy eyes could rest has vanished along with it, wallpaper with little pictures of people in folk costume. (Did I invent that? Was there really wallpaper like that in *our* planes?). I recall the sight of my countrymen shoving their belongings into the overhead bins to the rhythm of an Argentine tango, the sight of a young woman in fashionable skin-tight pants—white with large black dots—in high-heeled sandals, the little straps of the sandals revealing dry, cracked heels. The passengers cram in their cardboard boxes tied with coarse twine, they bluster, gesticulate, cast uneasy glances around, they sweat. The people fidget, stand up, sit down, call to each other, wave, take off their shoes to rest their tired feet, struggle with their luggage to the rhythm of an Argentine tango. Maybe I ought to have recognized in that scene of three years ago the massacres we have today, maybe I should have spotted today's horror in that confused scene of three years ago, the backstabbing behind those uneasy glances, the ravaged house behind the cardboard boxes done up with twine, today's conflagrations behind the calm smoke of a cigarette. Perhaps I should have recognized—in that sight of my sweaty, uneasy countrymen maneuvering in the narrow space of the aisle to the melody of the Argentine tango—the sea of refugees now winding its way on board sad trains through Europe. People entering countries in the lines labeled "other." Others, internationals, the embittered, the tough, those who cross borders with cardboard boxes done up with twine, those whose gazes hide misery, loss, hatred, and despair.

And I wonder whether, now that these things are so certain, I'll change my trajectory when I reach Amsterdam's Schiphol Airport. Instead of boarding the plane to Zagreb, will I have the nerve to board a different one? Because I shudder at my homeland. I shudder at the misery pouring into me these last months, concentrated in newspaper articles, television images, newspaper photographs, I shudder at the thought of the sorrows that have crawled toward me over phone lines, whiffs of the sadness that has reached me in letters. I shudder at the thought of my old homeland where I've become a stranger, which no longer even exists, I shudder at the thought of its ghost, I shudder at the thought of the new country where I'll be a stranger, whose citizenship I have yet to apply for, I'll have to prove I was born there, though I was, that I speak its language, though it is my mother tongue, I shudder at the thought of this old-new homeland for which I'll have to fight in order to live there—as a permanent émigré.

"Are you looking forward to going home?" asks the young woman in the seat beside me.

"No," I say bluntly and I see judgment in her eyes (how heartless she is, she thinks). At the same time I see her plucking from my heartlessness a sweet little berry, a point for herself (I could never say that, she thinks).

My heart is small and receptive. How many other people's sorrows can fit into one heart? How elastic is the average human heart? How much can fit in it without it bursting? Or does the heart after a certain time turn into a blunt little bellows blindly throbbing out its rhythm?

The route I take between leaving one plane and boarding the next, from gate to gate, from flight to flight, is a route of inner freedom. I ride along the moving walkway, quickening my pace, with the blue, green, and yellow arrows buffeting my face in a colored wind. Then I get off the walkway, walk, look at my watch. There is still a lot of time before the next flight. I settle into a comfortable airport seat and listen to the cooing loudspeaker with eyes shut. Would Mr. Fisher, traveling to Paris, please come to the information desk . . . Would Mr. Ivanov and Mr. Popov kindly make their way to the departure gate for their flight to Moscow . . .

I feel good here. I am a human larva. Here, in this no-man's-land, I'll weave my natural nest. I'll wander from sector A to sector B, from sector B to sector C. I'll never leave. They'll never find me. By day I'll ride along the moving walkways, pretending to be on my way somewhere, at night I'll curl up in an armchair and doze while waiting for a flight never to be announced. I'll observe the passengers; with time I'll come to know exactly who is traveling where, I'll learn to distinguish the faces; when I hear someone's name over the loudspeaker I'll know exactly what that person looks like. I'll live under the artificial airport lights like a postmodern exhibit, in transit, hunkering in an ideal shelter, in limbo, in an emotionally aseptic space. I'll be fine. And if I'm sometimes overcome by an oppressive claustrophobia, I'll not make for the nearest exit. I'll never leave.

"What would you like to drink?" asks the friendly flight attendant in Croatian.

"Orange juice, thank you," I reply in English, blushing.

"Where's the life vest?" I correct myself hastily by asking in Croatian. Again I blush because of the inanity of what I've said, I blush because of its suddenness, because of my unconscious mistake. I'd never asked such a question before, and where had that phrase, "life vest," come from, the first time I'd ever said it in Croatian, and what would I do with a life vest, anyway?

"Under your seat," she replies automatically and moves away.

I summon my medallion, I summon the little image of Manhattan, clutching for it like a straw. It has disappeared somewhere. Words are slowly disappearing as well. I'll change what words I have left at the border, like money, into other words. Or another kind of silence. I think about all this while the seconds tick by. For the time being I'm still aloft. There's still time before we touch down. I have faith in my heart, in the elasticity of its muscles. Besides, the life vest is here somewhere, under the seat.

1993

P.S.

1.

Well here I am, a quarter century after that last essay, when I was midair, with a life-vest under my seat and a few more minutes to go until we landed in Zagreb, holding on to the mouse-like thought that the heart muscle was the only thing I could have faith in. That pale image of Manhattan, which I summoned then as I clutched at it as if it were the straw that would keep me afloat, I keep today in the box of my imaginary treasures. Manhattan—my medallion; Manhattan—my bracelet; Manhattan—my earring . . .

Nationaliteit: geen was the first version of this book to appear in print in long ago 1993 in the Netherlands, the same year that the Croatian edition, *Američki fikcionar*, appeared. A year later the book came out in German with the title *My American Fictionary*, and in English with the title *Have a Nice Day: From the Balkan War to the American Dream*. Four titles for the one book!

There is a measure of consolation in the fact that the British and American editions shared the same cover: a photograph of a person, apparently diminutive in stature, wearing a Mickey Mouse mask. The person appears to have been photographed on the platform of a subway stop, with arrows showing the way to two exits. One leads out onto Main Street, Adventureland, and Frontierland, and the other to Fantasyland. Mickey Mouse has clearly chosen the exit for Fantasyland. The editor—the same one who changed the title (who justified his preference by insisting that no one would understand the word *fictionary*)—never said where the photograph was from. In London bookstores I found the book in the humor section, possibly because of the title and cover image. I never even looked for it in American bookstores. The book appeared for an instant and then breathed its last, like a mayfly, an insect belonging to the ephemeral group of water insects, the Ephemeroptera.

2.

Meanwhile the word *fictionary* has wormed its way into the Urban Dictionary. Here are several playful definitions from anonymous, amateur lexicographers:

- A word that means absolutely nothing (. . .). Best guess: a dictionary with fictitious words. The word "Fictionary" would be included in that dictionary.
- Fiction in your imagination (imaginary), ergo fictionary. *He wished for something so much that he believed it when in fact it was fictionary.*
- When something is both fiction and imaginary. *The story is about a fictionary town.*

- Words that are compounded within your brain which you entirely make up and which make no sense to other people. Other people also have their own fictionaries.
- Fake, not real, made up, invented or created out of thin air. Similar to fiction but a tad bit more high class/high brow. *You're really good at making up stories, you should be a fictionary writer.*

3.

This second American edition is different in some ways from the first: one essay has been dropped, another added, a third has been trimmed a bit. The opening motto was replaced by two others. The closing text, a letter to Norman written after my return to Zagreb, has been dropped. Why? Because when I read it again it seemed to be pulling the book more toward a "Croatian Fictionary"; I felt this was compromising the collection in the same way the new Croatian political reality has been compromising its population by turning them—ever since the time the *Fictionary* first came out—into its hostages. Who knows, perhaps this was decided not by me but by the mysterious diminutive figure sporting the Mickey Mouse mask, the figure who was choosing the exit for Fantasyland from the subway station.

4.

The point of republishing the book is to encourage a new reading of the earlier text, a dialog between two moments that are a quarter century apart. In my case, the question arises: between which two—or more—moments? Was it between my stay in Holland and the time I spent in America? Between the Croatian time and the American time? Between the time I spent traveling and the time I spent in America? Between my American time back then and subsequent American stays?

I'm reminded of a friend who, having read the English translation, said I use ellipses far too often. The three dots visually irritate the reader. She found they were an ugly "graphic tic." Right now I feel the graphic tic was an unconscious expression of the fact that a book like *American Fictionary* is open-ended and, furthermore, its open-endedness and scatter serve as a parallel theme throughout. Work on any text that has "lexicographical" pretensions, even when they are tongue-in-cheek, is unlikely ever to be finished.

5.

The innocent phrase *Have a Nice Day* from the title of the first English-language edition has meanwhile gone viral. Every country and every language has its own translated version today. Croats say: *Ugodan dan*, the Dutch, *Fijne dag*, the Bosnians, *Prijatan dan*, and the Swedes, *Ha en bra dag*. And the cadence of the phrase in America has, meanwhile, also changed, it has become darker and softer. That exaggerated yodel at the tail end of the phrase, which had always ended on an upward flip, now has dropped, crestfallen. The phrase is uttered today more evenly, more directly, with far less feigned enthusiasm than before.

6.

After my stay in America I returned to Zagreb. I imagined that my work on the essays for my American fictionary would be my way of sketching my homeward trajectory. Soon enough the opposite proved true: the essays were, instead, an introduction to a different sort of fictionary, to the exile on which I embarked in 1993, only a year after I'd returned from America. I'd come to feel afraid of my homeland, where I had become a stranger in a short time, where I had to prove I was born there, though I was born there, prove that I spoke its language, though it is my mother tongue. I was stricken with fear about the homeland for which I'd have to fight in order to win the status of a permanent émigré. My sudden fear about "landing" during the flight from New York to Zagreb in June of 1992 proved warranted.

7.

Every time over the last twenty-odd years when I've found myself in New York, I've gone to Central Park and had a look at 854 Fifth Avenue. This beautiful six-story building, which had belonged to an heiress of the Vanderbilt family, was purchased after her death by the SFRY, the Socialist Federal Republic of Yugoslavia. The building served as the seat of the Yugoslav Mission to the United Nations. Since the early 1990s, the grimy window panes and drawn curtains were all that could be seen. Although the building had belonged to Yugoslavia, the Serbian mission moved in when the country fractured. In November 2016, the former Yugoslav republics finally reached an agreement to sell the building. I don't know why, but I feel that with the sale of the building, Yugoslavia, the country I used to call my own, disappeared once and for all. This real estate detail encapsulates the story of the country's break-up: in the brutal theft of common property packaged in the version—more amenable to all—of ethnic hatred, in the supposed struggle against communist repression, in supposed democracy, in the supposed struggle for emancipation of national identity. But the conflict was, in fact, all about real estate.

I saw the building for the last time in October 2016, several days before the announcement that it would be sold. The windows were still grimy and the curtains drawn.

8.

Norman, who is mentioned in the book, married his Madeline. In late August 1993, just as I was leaving Zagreb, Norman arrived there as an official of the United Nations. Norman and Madeline lived in many parts of the former Yugoslavia, in Zagreb, Knin, Sarajevo, Tuzla, Skopje, Prizren . . . During the war, surrounded by a hatred that wasn't theirs, Norman and Madeline had three children. They returned to America, the children are now grown, and Norman and Madeline are divorced. He returned to the zone of his enduring fascination, the *former Yugoslavia,* where, as I write these lines, he now lives. His BCS (Bosnian, Croatian, Serbian) is impeccable, and his degree of knowledge about the region, as well as his tolerance for the same, are remarkable.

9.

After years of wandering I finally settled in Amsterdam, the first brief haven I'd set off from and the destination for my "messages in a bottle"—the essays that became the American fictionary. I have been living in Amsterdam now for twenty years.

During these years I've grown to feel that life in Amsterdam is like wearing comfy slippers. Having said that, I should add that Hotel New York in Rotterdam is one of my favorite watering holes in the Netherlands. The hotel stands on a pier that was the embarkation point during the nineteenth century for a host of émigrés who traveled from there to America on board the ships of the Holland America line. Although the powerful theme of the mass European exodus to America was never a part of my own story, I experience this place as a vortex of the yarn-spinning historical imagination.

In my quarter of Amsterdam, a neighborhood has emerged called "New York." Furthermore, across the street from it loom large buildings—tall by Amsterdam standards—that have acquired the moniker of "Little Manhattan." Countries and cities, exactly like people, lead secret lives, they exchange compliments and barbs. Cities, like people, send one another messages of love, they often grow larger purely out of spite, send one another nods of recognition, correct historical blunders . . . Powerful New York was born as the Dutch colony of New Amsterdam. The residents of these cities have long since forgotten this episode, but perhaps the cities themselves have not! Maybe this is why Amsterdam is now going all out to remind New York of the bond of years past, at least in the way they are naming the new neighborhoods and buildings. The Netherlanders are standing on their tiptoes, sending an air kiss across the mighty ocean to that city that is also theirs, New York.

10.

In the intervening years I have been to America many times. America does not have only one face, nor are all Americans the same, nor does the designation "American" hold any meaning at all. Truths such as these have been worn thin with over-repetition. The truths, however, are repeated because there are good reasons to do so. One of these is forgetting, the second is the need for us to remind ourselves of the oh so fragile institution of political correctness. I still think that any self-respecting author should steer clear of writing autobiography, diaries, and, especially, texts about other countries. All three smack of narcissism, the basic premise of every literary act, but they shouldn't also be its outcome. And in all three genres this outcome is a challenge to avoid. For all of us, almost without exception, are clandestine conquerors, everything we touch we turn into our "colony." Tourists are little more than innocent colonizers who, instead of native skulls, bring home symbolic substitutes: a key ring with a little yellow New York taxi, an *I love NY* mug, a snow globe with a miniature Empire State Building . . .

Once, on my way back from a stay in Chapel Hill, North Carolina, I brought home a suitcase packed with folders. In the folders I had carefully arranged leaves, the most beautiful autumn leaves I'd ever seen, and which I'd toted home like a precious trophy. I was smuggling American autumn into European territory. I still, today, feel a flush of embarrassment at the thought that the customs officials might have opened my suitcase . . .

11.

Everything in the essay "Shrink" is invented. The only true part is my edgy, double-seeing angle on the world. One angle faces inward, anxious and dark; the other is outward, cheery and bright—chasing playfully after the balls bouncing into focus.

The "virus," the "epicenter," the feeling of the fragility of everything surrounding me dogged me for a long time. At the moment when, utterly paralyzed, I watched the Twin Towers come down on my television screen, I felt the whole world was crumbling. From that moment on, *anything* was possible, moreover *everything* began speeding up. There is violence daily, a bomb explodes somewhere, a maniac somewhere brandishes a machete, dagger, or axe in a public place, someone blows himself up with a suicide bomb, taking with him to death a crowd of people. We have all grown accustomed to scrambling to our feet, mentally brushing off the dust, thanking whoever each one of us thanks that we have survived (again!) and moving on, while forgetting the next second what just happened. We're living in a war, everyone is at war with everyone else. And that same epicenter dogging the Montenegrin shepherd wherever he went is still dogging me, all of us.

12.

My friends, the people with whom I exchanged those long letters, are alive, living all over the world. Today we no longer write each other letters. Instead we send off the occasional email, seldom longer than a brief sentence or two. As an excuse for the long delay in responding we rely on technological hypocrisy: either our mail or theirs ended up in the spam folder. Between birth and death stretches spam. We have changed, one way or another. Meanwhile we have all waded into the post-human age, we're hooked up to electronic devices, to computers, iPhones, iPads, Kindles, to step trackers, social networks, Twitters, heart-rate trackers, and we know each other less and less. With startling ease we amputate our connections without thinking that we're hurting one another, because they are cutting us off with such ease, without thinking they're hurting us. Connect—disconnect, in—out, on—off . . . We are flooded by a feeling of power, we're convinced that we control our "property," and, hey, we're all more and more lonely.

Meanwhile, Yugoslavia went from being the "country where there's a war on" to being Slovenia, Croatia, Bosnia and Herzegovina, Serbia, Macedonia, Montenegro, and Kosovo. Our clothes often outlive us, but occasionally our homeland predeceases us. My mother, who "collected other people's deaths, rattling them mournfully like coins in a piggy bank," is also no longer among the living.

13.

After rereading it, I noticed that the *America* of my fictionary was fast becoming *New York*, though I wasn't even aware I'd been betraying the title.

E. B. White—author of what is probably the shortest book about New York, *Here is New York*, published in 1949—describes three New Yorks. "There is, first, the New York of the man or woman who was born here, who takes the city for granted and accepts its size and its turbulence as natural and inevitable. Second, there is the New York of the commuter—the city that is devoured by locusts each day and spat out each night. Third, there is the New York of the person who was born somewhere else and came to New York in quest of something. Of these three trembling cities the greatest is the last—the city of final destination, the city that is a goal. (. . .) Commuters gives the city its tidal restlessness; natives give it solidity and continuity; but the settlers give it passion."

I don't exactly belong in any of these three categories, though I do have a little something of each, even the one which, in my case, is the least convincing, that of the New York old-timer. Having stayed in the city for brief periods—most often with friends, less often in hotels, at addresses all over Manhattan, Brooklyn, and Queens, for three decades—I have learned something about the body and the city, especially about urban physicality, about the ecstasy of the shared dweller-city rhythm, about the betrayal of the rhythm, about slowing down, about the poignancy of reconciling to the fact that the body is aging, about physical inadequacy, about the distances we cover with ease in our youth until at a point they become undoable, about the rhythm of the city's pulse and the pulse of the heart, about physical cunning, about a premeditated stroll (which subway stop has only stairs for access, which has an elevator and escalators?), the movie theaters with, of late, incredibly comfortable seating, seats that can recline to become a bed, about the foot-massage salons that allow walk-ins where spry Chinese women relieve the pain in our feet so we can proceed on our way, about the rich imagination spurred by the experience of the body traversing city space, about the enchanting "transport" myths of popular culture (Superman! Batman! Spider-man!), which spring from the longing of the body for metamorphosis, for a body entirely attuned to the demands of a city like New York, about the inventions of urban architecture that respond to the same longing (such as High Line Park, where we feel as if we're walking among rooftops, water tanks, and terraces). A friend of mine, a New Yorker, says she has trained her body so that, if need be, she can walk from her office in Manhattan to her home in Brooklyn. She developed this sort of physical stamina after September 11. Petite, sylphlike, equipped with a small backpack that has become one with her body, she strides like a female samurai, she has taken the measurements, length and width, and wears the city like clothing. New York is just her size. Now *there's* a New Yorker. She has earned her New York. I, in contrast, have not. I am merely an observer, a writer, a high risk. Because all I have is the view, whether wrong or distorted, focused or loose, addled or clear, this view or that.

14.

Much has, meanwhile, changed. The phone booths—an essential part of American everyday life, both life as it really was and the life portrayed in movies and myth—are gone from the urban landscape. The newspaper kiosks, too, are gone. There are still kiosks to be found, but they mostly sell trinkets and bottled beverages, which means that in an evolutionary sense we are moving more and reading less, and if we do read, we aim to do so on the move, easily and quickly, most often on the screens of our cell phones.

New York has, meanwhile, grown to be even more beautiful. The skyscrapers in Queens and New Jersey now compete with Manhattan's. On Manhattan, meanwhile, new skyscrapers have shot up as slender as pencils. Owned, they say, by the Chinese, with one apartment per floor. In May 2017, I went up the Empire State Building, something I'd done only once before during my first visit to New York. From there New York looks like a box full of pencils. Instead of yesteryear's PAN AM ads, the most visible were now the red letters of H&M.

15.

My twenty-year-old nephew, for whom Starbucks, no matter where he goes, serves as his compass, recently read my essay on the bagel. "You are so heartless about the muffin. I think an apology is in order," said this young man, speaking for his age group. True, a person ought to tread with extreme caution, as if walking on eggs. I also owe an apology to the doughnut since the doughnut came to America with the Dutch, known as the *oliekoeck*, evolving, in America, from the sweet, deep-fried, doughy ball into the ring-shape we know so well. Cookies and coleslaw also came to America with the Dutch, the etymology of the word "cookie" is the venerable Dutch word *koekjen*, while coleslaw is an anglicized version of Dutch *koolsla*.

My nephew knows nothing about how the English muffin was invented by Samuel Bath Thomas, an emigrant from Plymouth, who—upon arriving in New York—opened a bakery. The Thomas muffin is something altogether different from the ones about which I was so, apparently, heartless. Thanks to my publisher, I now have the opportunity to make amends. Moved by my nephew's compassion and by my respect for minority versus majority opinion, I hereby apologize to the muffin, that freak of flour, that culinary curiosity that erased Thomas's respectable innovation from the list of baked goods, stealing even its name. My apologies to the quick bread admired only by ignoramuses and amateurs, the crumb that fancied itself a cake, the baking-powder junkie, the repast of infantile and indolent chewers, the con artist that inveigled its way in among the rolls, the fraud, the lack of culinary imagination, the edible entity with no flavor or flair, the floury zero . . .

16.

Since that long-ago 1991 when I found myself in New York in mid-October, when a war that would last for the next four years was just beginning in my homeland, I have been without a homeland. I have a home, though not in the country where I was born, so I am not homeless. I have a passport and a tax ID number, so I am not stateless, nor am I country-less. The condition of "exhausting mental and emotional simultaneity," the "frenzied crisscrossing of parallel worlds," with which I diagnosed myself in 1991 at the time of the war in Yugoslavia and my sojourn in America, became, in time, my lifestyle. As I travel I collect places, people, and situations as if they are souvenir-substitutes for a "homeland." All these places (people and situations) stir in me a feeling that eludes translation into language. The feeling is closer to melancholy than nostalgia, closer to a presentiment than regret. The most compelling part is how arbitrary this is. I can never predict what this feeling will evoke, just as I don't know whether I am a hunter out to snare capricious "homeland" sentiments or I am their prey, whether I'm the "adopter" or the "adoptee."

So it was that I recently happened to find myself in the town of Norman, Oklahoma. I was put up there for a few days in a homey sort of inn (is there such a hospitality category as world-class emotional accommodation?), an old wooden house with a veranda, an overgrown garden out back, and a rusty table and chairs in the garden. When I came out in my pajamas one early October morning onto the veranda, I sat on the porch swing and sipped at my warm coffee. Through the screen I surveyed the surrounding landscape: the overgrown front garden, neighboring houses, the completely empty street . . . Everything had been wreathed by a mist that would gradually acquire a golden haze, promising a warm and sunny day. And then the wail of a train's whistle cut through the stillness, a sound I hadn't heard since my childhood. This was an auditory reminder that trains passed through the town but didn't stop. Enchanted by the air, as sweet and fragrant as an overripe melon, I felt as if here, on this porch, on the swing, wrapped in stillness and the golden haze, I could stay forever. That veranda is my "homeland."

17.

American melancholy lurks in a space marked by antonyms, contrasts. Melancholy may pounce in a surprise attack at a moment in a major department store, or in a vast supermarket where the sheer quantity of merchandise sends us spinning into a panic attack, at a chic boutique of a big-brand fashion designer where we stop to stare at things as if hypnotized. And so it was that I stopped for a moment at the Louis Vuitton store on Fifth Avenue (it could have been anywhere, because the "world of elegance, inspiration, and imagination" has gone, as they say, global). I stared, transfixed, at the price tag on an ordinary cosmetics bag; they were asking the same amount for it as the advance I'd received for my most recent book. I stood there, confronted by the fact that my many years of work on the book (how pathetic does that sound!) were worth, on the open market, the same as a Vuitton cosmetics bag . . . (Sorry? No, it was not studded with rubies . . . Yes, an ordinary little bag for makeup! No, it was not, as far as I could tell, made of leather . . . Yes, it had the LV initials and little stars and dots on it . . . No, it was certainly not a man's wallet! No, this was no evening bag! Yes, an ordinary one, for makeup . . . Jesus Christ, I know what a bag for cosmetics looks like! What? How long is my novel? Over three hundred pages, but what does that have to do with anything, for God's sake?)

The same sort of melancholy came over me at a farm in Oklahoma when my friends and I lost our way, mistakenly turning off the right road onto the wrong exit. And here, under the dome of the sky, sat a man out in front of his house on a rocking chair. The man was utterly alone, there was nobody else there, not even a dog, the sounds were completely hushed, the dome of the sky high above, crystal clear and blue. The man sat in the surreal landscape, before him a makeshift stand; it was Sunday and the man had brought out things he was hoping to get rid of. For fifty cents I bought a miniature drawer. The drawer had belonged, I assume, to a cheap jewelry box. Having clinched the utterly senseless transaction, I felt as if I were in a parallel reality, for at this spot where nobody came, nobody passed through, nobody stopped, at this pint-sized flea market open to the skies, God would stop by—if there is a God—only when he was bored to death.

I wondered momentarily whether the stand amid the vast horizon and under the dome of empty sky was the beginning or end of the trajectory of the Vuitton cosmetics bag, or both, which hardly matters anyway as the Earth is round, and we, on Earth, are troubled by metaphysical emptiness, just as is He or She who, they say, created us in his or her own image. All else is stuffing. And Vuitton's bag is here to stuff a hole.

18.

Of all the cities the world over where I have been until now, I have felt the least lonely in New York. When I spend a few days or longer in any part of New York, I first plant my flag. My high-priority territories are the hair and nail salons. And when the same establishment houses both that is, of course, better yet. In New York one also finds the small services, the dry cleaners and seamstresses, owned by chronically taciturn Chinese. I use whatever excuse I can come up with: this needs hemming, this lengthening, because the clothing item isn't important, it's all about marking territory: this is *my* dry cleaner, *my* seamstress.

The hair and nail salons are places of vital importance. Those that offer the least expensive services are the ones worth finding. Why? Because those are where the new arrivals, the freshest emigrants, work. These salons are better than UN agencies or any of the other institutions studying migration, because the information available to the salon is far more current.

So here I am in *my* hair salon in Brooklyn. I don't know the women, they're new. My ear catches a language I don't recognize.
"What language is that?" I ask.

"Russian."

"It can't be Russian," I say in my fluent (of that I'm sure!) Russian.

"That is how we, Jews from Bukhara, speak Russian," they say.

I was in that remarkable city briefly a long time ago—during the Soviet days. The hammer and sickle and red star never made their way into this walled, fairy-tale city: communism ruled on the outside, and ancient customs reigned inside. At the Bukhara bazaar they used to say—under communism—that you could buy hashish, frequently concealed in tastefully carved dried gourds. I didn't buy any, but I did have a puff or two during a visit to the long-gone USSR. Leonid Brezhnev was head of state.

The girls chatted among themselves, but now they were speaking something else.

"What language is that now?"

"Hebrew . . . "

"It doesn't sound like Hebrew to me, I was in Jerusalem just a month ago," I say. Good lord, I think, what a tiresome stickler I am.

"That's the way we, Jews from Bukhara, speak Hebrew," the women answer politely.

I hear these women have just arrived, they left Bukhara because they could no longer stand the "aggressive Islamization of the country." Do they have PhDs in political science? I wonder briefly. I learn they are living in Queens, where a small Jewish Uzbek colony thrives.

"But now here they are, coming after us," said one of them.

"Who is coming after you?"

"The Muslims, of course!"

"Why?"

"Because they, too, can't stand the aggressive Islamization of Uzbekistan," they say and giggle.

Candy is here, too, a Brazilian woman with a sugarcoated name and expertise in threading. Threading is the plucking of facial hair using a thin thread. Candy is a master of this ancient craft, which, they say, comes to us from India. She holds one end of the thread between her teeth and the other between her fingers which she maneuvers adeptly to pluck the little hairs quickly out by the roots, exactly as if picking a tiny turnip. The focus of Candy's treatment is mainly the eyebrows, though there are hairs which need to be kept in line on other parts of the body. Among her customers she works on men as often as women. I watch them sitting there, faces solemn, as if they were undergoing a life-or-death operation, and then they get up out of Candy's chair, armed with eyebrows like little machetes, ready to confront the world. "Oh, everybody knows you can spot Brooklynites by their eyebrows!" says a friend and it is up to me to decide whether I believe him or not. It may well be that Candy is practicing "Brazilian voodoo," using the eyebrows as her excuse. For who knows what it is she is truly tying and untying, whom she's joining and separating, and with whose destinies she meddles.

Life in New York is an unending and inexhaustible orgy of communication. The party begins in the cab that brings me into town from the airport. All the New York dwellers, be they old-timers, newcomers, or passersby, are part of the conversation, like it or not, and they often seem intoxicated by it, hurtling into verbal embrace with strangers, exactly as if there hadn't been a living soul on their horizon for years. I submit happily to the orgy of communication, feeling myself charge up with power like a battery long drained.

Sometimes I need a break and sit on a chair or bench along a street somewhere, a spot engaged in the pretense of garden restoration: a few tables and chairs, trees growing from soil-filled concrete tubs. Last time I stopped by the garden of the Museum of Modern Art, ringed by skyscrapers with a few potted trees and shrubs, a little fountain, and a changing display of sculptures. I perched on a wire-mesh garden chair by a sculpture, an immense metal rose that shot upward with an open red, metal blossom. I sat and thought about how this garden, despite the constant flow of visitors, is always quiet. And then toward me began to creep mysterious sounds of the jungle, the chirping of birds coming from speakers concealed in the treetops, shrubs, and flower beds. The sounds would wax for a moment, then wane again, then wax like the ebb and flow of the tides. Later I learned this was *Birdcalls*, a sound installation by New York artist Louise Lawler. I sat there for a long while, captivated by the sounds, motionless, ensnared in a time and sound warp.

19.

I don't know why, but for the last few years I have been writing the date on each text I write, in each book I buy, exactly as if leaving bread crumbs in the hope that, should I lose my way, somebody could find me. My effort does not make much sense, because nothing, including history, proceeds in a linear fashion, everything "moves in loops, tropes, inversions of meaning."

In May 2017, on a stone bench on Fifth Avenue, with the Plaza Hotel in the background, somewhere along the "familial" diagonal linking the hotel Ivana used to run with Donald's tower, sat a panhandler, in a business-like suit and tie, wearing a Donald Trump mask. He might well have been an actor, the New York panhandlers are often the finest entertainers. Next to him on the pavement was a small container for loose change and a cardboard sign announcing: "Donate! Collecting money to build the Mexico wall." The cheerful man caught my gaze and boldly gave me a thumbs-up. I returned the gesture, sure that we were exchanging a message with the same meaning. Down with Trump, down with walls!

Concepts, by the way, change meaning. We have found ourselves snarled in a semantic traffic jam and we'll have a difficult time finding our way out. There is no end to the prefix "post," everything is suddenly post-something: post-national, post-colonial, post-independence, post-totalitarian, post-identity, post-trauma, post-Yugoslav, postindustrial, post-communism, post-socialism, post-capitalism, post-history, postmortem, postmodernism, post-postmodernism, post-human, post-apocalyptic, post-truth, post-fiction, pre-post-fiction, post-dictionary, post-fictionary . . .

20.

If I were to write the American fictionary again, the word to hold pride of place would be "island." Not any island, but a specific one. Roosevelt Island. I find it interesting that none of my New York friends had ever set foot on it though it is right there in front of them. Roosevelt Island is a slender swath of land lying in the middle of East River between Manhattan and Queens (or Long Island). The swath is two miles long and, at most, 800 feet wide. From above it looks, I'd say, like an anchored barge. The island has changed names, much as my book has changed titles. The first name on record was a Native American one: Minnehanonck or "nice island." Indians hunted, fished, and gathered berries here, until the first Dutch settlers arrived in 1623. Wouter Van Twiller became the Dutch governor in 1633 and persuaded the Indians to sell him the island. It was used thereafter as a place to raise pigs for the tables of the Dutch settlers, and for that reason they called it Varkens Eylandt, Hog Island. When the English came into power, Captain John Manning, the New York sheriff, was given the island as his reward for loyalty to the English Crown, and the name the island was given was, predictably: Manning's Island. After Manning's death the island was inherited by his adopted daughter, who was married to Robert Blackwell. The name was then changed to Blackwell's Island and this name stuck until 1921 when, because of its purpose, it was rechristened Welfare Island. The name Roosevelt Island, after Franklin Delano Roosevelt, dates from 1971. The islanders seldom call it by its name, referring to it instead as "the island," or "our island."

Roosevelt Island lies spitting distance from Manhattan, stretching from 46th to 85th Streets, 39 blocks long. There is an F-line subway stop on the island, and Queensboro Bridge is there for the cars, but the fastest and most enjoyable way to get there is the tramway that runs from the island to 59th Street, taking only four minutes of soaring through the air. The trip from Roosevelt Island to Manhattan is spectacular. Equally spectacular is the view of Manhattan from the island in any season, and at any time of day or night. All of Roosevelt Island is a "room with a view," it is the distance one needs, a place where there is always air to breathe before we fling ourselves into Manhattan's embrace. Roosevelt Island is a slow-motion frame, that moment for contemplation before crystalizing a decision. Roosevelt Island is a teaser, a lure that only sharpens our taste for Manhattan. We can, of course, decide, in anger, that we aren't going over there today and linger instead on the Meditation Steps where we'll let ourselves be seduced by the glittering sight on the other riverbank—Emerald City. Here, on the spacious wooden steps, much like an open-air theater, we'll recline with an arm as a pillow. Manhattan will pant and lick us like a devoted dog. The day will be warm and we'll slip off into a dream like Dorothy, dazed in the poppy field.

By 1820 the number of New Yorkers had risen to an incredible 123,706, and with this surge in population came crime, disease, and poverty. The Blackwell family sold the island to the government of the city of New York, which decided to move its "unhealthier" inhabitants there. The symbolic foundation of the island's new social organization was laid when a prison was built there in 1832. Then they built the New York City Lunatic Asylum, an architectural gem in the shape of an octagon, in 1841. A prison hospital for patients afflicted with venereal disease was later built, then a poor house, a reformatory, and a minimum-security prison for petty criminals, mainly prostitutes and drunks. The Smallpox Hospital opened in 1856. It was closed in the late nineteenth century after effective vaccinations had been discovered, but in 1902 it was renovated to become the New York School of Nursing. Eleven institutions were begun by 1872; of them, today, the protected ruins of the famous Octagon remain.

Although the island served as a quarantine for medical, social, and prison isolation, a place for dumping "human refuse," its activities and services were no secret. Having arrived in America in 1842, Charles Dickens visited the island asylum and was moved both by the stunning architectural details and the appalling treatment of patients. Nelly Bly, an American journalist and pioneer of investigative reporting, feigned insanity so that she could be institutionalized. Once she'd succeeded, she wrote a series of articles that were published in 1887 as the book *Ten Days in a Mad-House*. The book kicked up dust and forced the authorities to improve the life of patients in psychiatric wards, as well as to subject psychiatrists to supervision and control.

The island prison became known for celebrated prisoners. Emma Goldman was imprisoned here for espousing anarchism and the legalization of abortion, as was Madame Restell for practicing abortion. Ida Craddock was sentenced to the island for her sexual manuals, particularly *The Wedding Night*. She refused to be declared mad, which would have spared her incarceration. After she was released, charges were raised yet again for the same book, which was, in the opinion of the judges, unforgivably obscene, lewd, lascivious, and dirty. This time

Ida was sentenced to five years, but instead of prison she chose suicide. Billie Holiday was jailed here for prostitution. Becky Edelsohn, an anarchist, was jailed for taking part in demonstrations against John D. Rockefeller, whom she declared a multi-murderer, saying the city was his property and calling on people to tear down the capitalist system. Mae West stayed briefly at the island jail because of *Sex*, a play that premiered on Broadway in 1927. As co-author and producer of the play she was sentenced to ten days in jail, but was released three days early for good behavior. Mae West donated the money she earned from an article she wrote about her stay in the Roosevelt Island jail to fund the beginnings of the Memorial Prison Library.

21.

During my most recent visit to New York, I sat there at my favorite spot on the Roosevelt Island Meditation Steps. It was late afternoon, Manhattan was sinking into darkness across the water. From my backpack I had taken the book, the second edition of which you hold in your hands. I'd thought to leaf through it and plan how to begin this post scriptum. Instead I left it shut and sat back to watch Manhattan bask in the last rays of sun as boats plied through the murky waters of the East River.

When I returned home to the apartment where I was a guest, only a five-minute walk from the Meditation Steps, I noticed I no longer had my book. I went back, but couldn't find it. Someone had already picked it up. I imagined who that might be . . . One of the many young Chinese people I'd met on the free shuttle bus that runs between the subway station and the tramway? A former compatriot? On the island there is, I believe, a colony more numerous than the "little Balkans" of Astoria. Was the book picked up by the Japanese waitress at Fuji East Bistro? Or Alina—the Russian hairdresser from Fusion Salon on Main Street?

Meanwhile a warm twilight had descended, and I sat again on the steps, watching, enchanted, as the lights went on in Manhattan. I thought about how every time I come to New York I play the same game: I leave things behind, sometimes I forget them on purpose, sometimes by chance. How many American friends have I supplied with hairdryers they don't need? Americans seldom use them, so I buy one and leave it behind, why drag such things back and forth to Europe. I leave shoes, slippers, towels, toothbrushes, T-shirts, umbrellas, books, jackets . . . the jackets I usually forget in taxis. I leave my things behind as a pledge to return; if I leave nothing behind, who knows if I'd ever come back. I stare at the lights of Manhattan and think about how forgetting the book on the steps was exactly the right end to this day. Everything in New York is interconnected. Even the most distant worlds are connected by secret threads. The people who swiftly spin the little balls, covering them with cups, the seedy slice of humanity that draws the gazers of passersby, that enchants, cheats, performs their cheap skill, and, without knowing it, spins the world . . . With one end of the thread between her teeth and the other between her fingers, Candy's hands adeptly flash scissor-like and shape the eyebrows of many a Brooklynite. The Brazilian woman with the sugarcoated name knows her craft, and there you have it, all her eyebrows resemble miniature machetes shielding the owner from curses and keeping enemies at bay. In the soft New York night, cat shadows slink through the city, scratching and purring, tying threads into little knots of destiny. In the soft New York night the stars clink like tokens, pass quietly from pocket to pocket, and twinkle like the smiles of the passersby. Manhattan sparkles like a magical puzzle. Somewhere along the border between sleep and waking a balance is struck, somewhere all debts are paid, black is white, white is black, gain is loss, loss is gain. By leaving things behind I, too, am performing my own childish voodoo, insuring my next visit, my next spell of New York enchantment.

I also think a moment about my book, about the person who picked it up on that late May afternoon in 2017 from the Meditation Steps on "our island." Then I unleash my imagination and picture the ghosts of the women imprisoned here, lifting my book from the wooden steps; the book floats up—borne aloft by their breath—vibrating like a tiny glider mid-air . . . I imagine the ghosts of the women, the anarchists, prostitutes, thieves, entertainers, alcoholics, beggars, losers, lunatics, patients, renegades, and outcasts who smuggle my book into another time, into the Memorial Prison Library, the one founded by Mae West with the money she was paid for the article she wrote about her brief stay there. I imagine my book traveling back through time. All the books of this world, even the ones that speak of the future, come to us from the past, whether this be the past of yesterday, or one that reaches further back, or a time completely apart from us. And my book, borne by the breath of the unhappy women of the past, drops onto the shelf of the prison library like a frozen sparrow arriving from the future.

2017

Dubravka Ugresic is the author of seven works of fiction, including *The Museum of Unconditional Surrender* and *Baba Yaga Laid an Egg*, along with six collections of essays, including *Thank You for Not Reading* and *Karaoke Culture*, a finalist for the National Book Critics Circle Award for Nonfiction. She has won, or been shorlisted for, more than a dozen prizes, including the NIN Award, Austrian State Prize for European Literature, Heinrich Mann Prize, *Independent* Foreign Fiction Prize, Man Booker International Prize, and the James Tiptree Jr. Award. In 2016, she received the Neustadt International Prize for Literature (the "American Nobel") for her body of work.

Celia Hawkesworth is the translator of numerous works of Serbian, Croatian, and Bosnian literature, including Dubravka Ugresic's *The Culture of Lies*, for which she won the Heldt Prize for Translation in 1999.

Ellen Elias-Bursać has been translating fiction and nonfiction by Bosnian, Croatian, and Serbian writers since the 1980s, including novels and short stories by David Albahari, Dubravka Ugresic, Daša Drndić, and Karim Zaimović. She is co-author of a textbook for the study of Bosnian, Croatian, and Serbian with Ronelle Alexander, and author of *Translating Evidence and Interpreting Testimony at a War Crimes Tribunal: Working in a Tug-of-War*, which was awarded the Mary Zirin Prize in 2015.

Inga Ābele (Latvia)
High Tide
Naja Marie Aidt (Denmark)
Rock, Paper, Scissors
Esther Allen et al. (ed.) (World)
The Man Between: Michael Henry Heim & a Life in Translation
Bae Suah (South Korea)
A Greater Music
North Station
Svetislav Basara (Serbia)
The Cyclist Conspiracy
Guðbergur Bergsson (Iceland)
Tómas Jónsson, Bestseller
Jean-Marie Blas de Roblès (World)
Island of Point Nemo
Per Aage Brandt (Denmark)
If I Were a Suicide Bomber
Can Xue (China)
Frontier
Vertical Motion
Lúcio Cardoso (Brazil)
Chronicle of the Murdered House
Sergio Chejfec (Argentina)
The Dark
My Two Worlds
The Planets
Eduardo Chirinos (Peru)
The Smoke of Distant Fires
Marguerite Duras (France)
Abahn Sabana David
L'Amour
The Sailor from Gibraltar
Mathias Énard (France)
Street of Thieves
Zone
Macedonio Fernández (Argentina)
The Museum of Eterna's Novel
Rubem Fonseca (Brazil)
The Taker & Other Stories
Rodrigo Fresán (Argentina)
The Bottom of the Sky
The Invented Part
Juan Gelman (Argentina)
Dark Times Filled with Light
Georgi Gospodinov (Bulgaria)
The Physics of Sorrow
Arnon Grunberg (Netherlands)
Tirza
Hubert Haddad (France)
Rochester Knockings: A Novel of the Fox Sisters
Gail Hareven (Israel)
Lies, First Person
Angel Igov (Bulgaria)
A Short Tale of Shame
Ilya Ilf & Evgeny Petrov (Russia)
The Golden Calf
Zachary Karabashliev (Bulgaria)
18% Gray
Hristo Karastoyanov (Bulgaria)
The Same Night Awaits Us All
Jan Kjærstad (Norway)
The Conqueror
The Discoverer
Josefine Klougart (Denmark)
One of Us Is Sleeping
Carlos Labbé (Chile)
Loquela
Navidad & Matanza
Jakov Lind (Austria)
Ergo
Landscape in Concrete
Andreas Maier (Germany)
Klausen
Lucio Mariani (Italy)
Traces of Time
Amanda Michalopoulou (Greece)
Why I Killed My Best Friend
Valerie Miles (World)
A Thousand Forests in One Acorn: An Anthology of Spanish-Language Fiction
Iben Mondrup (Denmark)
Justine
Quim Monzó (Catalonia)
Gasoline
Guadalajara
A Thousand Morons

WWW.OPENLETTERBOOKS.ORG

OPEN
LETTER

Elsa Morante (Italy)
Aracoeli
Giulio Mozzi (Italy)
This Is the Garden
Andrés Neuman (Spain)
The Things We Don't Do
Jóanes Nielsen (Faroe Islands)
The Brahmadells
Madame Nielsen (Denmark)
The Endless Summer
Henrik Nordbrandt (Denmark)
When We Leave Each Other
Wojciech Nowicki (Poland)
Salki
Bragi Ólafsson (Iceland)
The Ambassador
Narrator
The Pets
Kristín Ómarsdóttir (Iceland)
Children in Reindeer Woods
Diego Trelles Paz (ed.) (World)
The Future Is Not Ours
Ilja Leonard Pfeijffer (Netherlands)
Rupert: A Confession
Jerzy Pilch (Poland)
The Mighty Angel
My First Suicide
A Thousand Peaceful Cities
Rein Raud (Estonia)
The Brother
Mercè Rodoreda (Catalonia)
Death in Spring
The Selected Stories of Mercè Rodoreda
War, So Much War
Milen Ruskov (Bulgaria)
Thrown into Nature
Guillermo Saccomanno (Argentina)
Gesell Dome
Juan José Saer (Argentina)
The Clouds
La Grande
The One Before
Scars
The Sixty-Five Years of Washington
Olga Sedakova (Russia)
In Praise of Poetry
Mikhail Shishkin (Russia)
Maidenhair
Sölvi Björn Sigurðsson (Iceland)
The Last Days of My Mother
Maria José Silveira (Brazil)
Her Mother's Mother's Mother and Her Daughters
Andrzej Sosnowski (Poland)
Lodgings
Albena Stambolova (Bulgaria)
Everything Happens as It Does
Benjamin Stein (Germany)
The Canvas
Georgi Tenev (Bulgaria)
Party Headquarters
Dubravka Ugresic (Europe)
Europe in Sepia
Fox
Karaoke Culture
Nobody's Home
Ludvík Vaculík (Czech Republic)
The Guinea Pigs
Jorge Volpi (Mexico)
Season of Ash
Antoine Volodine (France)
Bardo or Not Bardo
Post-Exoticism in Ten Lessons, Lesson Eleven
Radiant Terminus
Eliot Weinberger (ed.) (World)
Elsewhere
Ingrid Winterbach (South Africa)
The Book of Happenstance
The Elusive Moth
To Hell with Cronjé
Ror Wolf (Germany)
Two or Three Years Later
Words Without Borders (ed.) (World)
The Wall in My Head
Xiao Hong (China)
Ma Bo'le's Second Life
Alejandro Zambra (Chile)
The Private Lives of Trees